Until We Meet Again

Last time we met for 54 years.
Next time – for eternity !

Thomas Toren

BALBOA.
PRESS

A DIVISION OF HAY HOUSE

Balboa Press books may be ordered through booksellers or by contacting:

Balboa Press
A Division of Hay House
1663 Liberty Drive
Bloomington, IN 47403
www.balboapress.com.au
1 (877) 407-4847

Printed in the United States of America.

ISBN: 978-1-4525-2679-9 (sc)

Balboa Press rev. date: 12/12/2014

This is a fascinating story, both as a personal journey of an individual who lived during extraordinary times, and as a historical document of that period. Tom describes aspects of life in pre-war Berlin, and subsequent escape from Nazi Germany to Harbin/China, where he lived with his step-father and sister during and after the Second World War under the Japanese and Soviet Russian occupation. He subsequently managed to leave the communist block by migrating to Israel, where Tom faced many new challenges, including army bureaucracy, the rigors of studying and trying to make ends meet. It was here that Tom met his beloved wife Lisa, and started his career, initially in mechanical engineering, and subsequently as an inventor. Tom describes in captivating detail the many aspects of his personal experiences, from his childhood relationships with his beloved mother and cold step-father, to his subsequent career success as consulting engineer and brilliant inventor in Australia. It is both an absorbing personal story and a remarkable historical document. I recommend it most highly to readers who enjoy biographies and discovering aspects of contemporary history.
-Sarah Edelman PhD
Author and Clinical Psychologist

Tom Toren shares with his readers his remarkable and inspiring journey of optimism, self-discipline, perseverance and professional creativity, as a twentieth century victim from Germany via Russia, China and, finally, Australia. His hard won freedom is a motivational force for his ongoing human rights activism!
-Dr Ellen M Campion

Contents

My Life Story

This is a short story of my long life, a life during which I covered a lot of territory, geographically speaking, and was fortunate enough to experience several very different cultures. However, as with everything in life, there was a price to pay for that "fortunate experience."

I dedicate this short story to my beloved wife and life's true friend, Lisa (who is waiting for me on the other side); to our wonderful daughter, Iris; and to our precious granddaughter, Laura, and her future children who may wonder what type of person their great-grandfather was and what strange experiences he may have had during his life.

Writing this account of my unusual life has also turned out to be a liberating, cathartic experience for me.

I hope you will enjoy reading it, both the sad and the funny bits. Thank you!

N.B.: Recently I was editing the draft of my life story whilst my car was being serviced. When the mechanic came to inform me that he had completed his job, he asked what I was writing. I told him that it was my life story. He asked, "Was it hard to write?" I hesitated, and then replied, "Writing it was easy; living it was hard." He understood—we both smiled.

Chapter 1

My Identity—Finally Resolved

I have had serious problems trying to establish my identity, especially during my childhood. As an adult, I accepted these problems, and only later in life was I able to resolve them.

Most people have no problems knowing who their parents are or what their nationalities and religions are. It all happens automatically for them.

Most people are born in the country that identifies their nationality and, if they so desire, they can spend their lives in their country of birth. In other words, they are born with a distinct identity, and they grow up with a sense of *belonging*. If they are lucky, they may even have good parents to support them in all that.

Many of us are not that lucky, at least with some of these important issues. Some of us miss out on all of these issues simply because, as Malcolm Fraser said, "life was not meant to be easy." A sense of *belonging* was always important to me, probably accentuated by the fact that I grew up without a mother and without a proper father; as such, I had *nobody* and *nothing* to belong to.

I know who my mother was, even though I grew up without her. I thought I knew who my father was, but fortunately, I realised later in life that he could not have been my biological father.

I was born in Berlin and was lucky to get out of there at the age of seven, shortly before the outbreak of World War II, so I certainly was not born in a country that I was able to identify with or had any desire to. My mother was born and grew up in Czestochowa within the Russian southern part of Poland in the late nineteenth century and moved to Germany after World War I.

As a small child, I was taken care of by my nanny, Froli, whom I loved very much. My mother, for some unknown reason, could not take care of me until I was five years old, which is when she officially divorced the man I had assumed to be my father. During the year that followed the divorce, I started developing a happy relationship with my mother at the fortnightly visitations to her new home. However, this relationship did not last long, because the Nazis arrested her for having a relationship with a Jew and put her in jail. (More about this later.) We left Berlin when she was still in prison. When I met my mother again twenty-two years later in London and Paris, and again in Germany during my frequent overseas business trips, a normal mother-and-son relationship could no longer be developed. In retrospect, this was primarily my fault because, unfortunately, being preoccupied with my work responsibilities, I did not take the opportunity of having a heart-to-heart discussion with her. I am sure she would have welcomed it, and during such an in-depth discussion, she probably would have told me who my biological father was.

As of 1938, after escaping from Berlin at the age of seven, I was lucky to grow up in the Russian immigrant community of Harbin, in the north of China. There I was brought up first by one Russian lady, Aleksandra Vakulovna, and then by another Russian lady, Lidia Ivanovna. Harbin had the largest Russian community outside Russia.

My stepfather was a German Jew, a doctor, and a good financial provider. I had nothing at all in common with him. I had to speak German with him during our limited daily interaction. His Prussian idea of bringing up a child consisted of instructions, discipline, and punishment. I grew up without parental love and without a role model.

I resolved my problems of identity when, as an adult, I realised that the father shown on my birth certificate could not have been my biological father. I accepted that I would not know who my father was until I meet my mother again on the "other side."

With my stepfather out of the picture, my Russian identity became crystal clear to me, which made me very happy, because the Russian language and Russian culture are what I grew up with and are the only culture that I can fully identify with. This sense of belonging was and is important to me. I have reason to believe that my biological father would have been either Polish or Russian.

It is also clear to me that the difference between people belonging to different nationalities is not due to their blood or genes. The difference is due to the culture in which they grew up, especially during their formative teenage years. Similarly, our daughter is not part Austrian and part Chinese like her mother, or Russian like me, or Israeli according to her country of birth; she is Australian because this is the country and culture where she grew up, where she was educated, and where she spent her formative years.

I have also resolved the question of my religion, but this happened only in later years, when I was already in my sixties and seventies. I had no religious upbringing as a child at a home without parents and in the Soviet Russian high school. However, it is my strong belief that if all of us would believe in and exercise the golden rule of "do unto others as you would have others do unto you," the world would be a far better place. It would be better still if all animals were to be included in the word *others*. I know that my wife, Lisa, our daughter, Iris, and our granddaughter, Laura, feel the same way about this. I also know that Laura will bring up her children with that commitment to justice and compassion for all.

Like her mother, Lisa was Jewish and, for at least ten last years of her life, she regularly visited the progressive Emanuel Synagogue to pray. Contrary to normal practice, Lisa only did so on weekdays. She was very friendly with the two rabbis, one of them a woman. Late last year, I visited the Emanuel Synagogue to look at the plaque that was put up for Lisa in the main hall. When I join Lisa, I would like this plaque to be replaced with a new one, bearing both our names. I have already discussed this with the staff of the synagogue. I spent about an hour praying in the synagogue that day. Because it was a Monday, I was the only person there, which felt good. The two rabbis, who remember Lisa fondly, were both present on another weekday when I was again praying in the synagogue. It happened two days before the second anniversary of Lisa's passing. As the two rabbis saw me enter the synagogue that day, they commented with a smile that I was upholding the Toren family tradition of praying on weekdays in solitude.

I like praying in churches of any Christian denomination, in Buddhist temples, and in synagogues, but only on weekdays, like Lisa did, when there are no religious services and no other people present. I find it easier to concentrate on my prayers in these houses of God than when doing so at home. There is only one God for all of us and for all of these temples and churches, and it is to Him that my prayers are directed. God has not created these religious divisions; they were created by people.

I should also mention that my mother was not Jewish. She christened me, as documented on my birth certificate, whilst my stepfather/doctor had me circumcised by one of his colleagues. I do not know which came first. One or both of them must have done so out of spite (*dafka*). In 1949, at the age of eighteen, I converted to Judaism, which enabled me to escape from the Communist world to Israel. Whilst living in Israel for thirteen years (in those early years of the Jewish state of Israel), I was aware of the fact that being Israeli added another dimension to being Jewish.

I should probably also mention that my primary, secondary, and tertiary education happened in four different languages: German, English, Russian, and Hebrew, in that order, which may have also contributed to my past identity issues. More details appear in the chapters that follow, where I shall elaborate on the issues raised here.

I would like to finish this introductory chapter on a positive note by saying that all the problems and difficulties I experienced in my childhood and youth must have made me stronger, more determined, and self-reliant. As I am writing this, it also occurs to me that it has left me with a few rather unusual advantages:

- When I am amongst Germans, they assume that I am one of them because I speak their language without an accent.
- When I am amongst Russians, I feel at home amongst my people.
- When I am amongst Israelis, I am accepted as an Israeli.
- When I am amongst Australians, I am accepted as an Australian, a product of our multicultural society.
- However, when I am at home by myself, listening to my iTunes collection of classical music and beautiful old Russian songs, I am still a Russian and will always be one.

In my forties, I must have gradually and subconsciously adopted a very positive approach when suddenly faced with life's minor or major problems—of which, as we know, there are many throughout life. Whenever something unpleasant or truly bad happens, I straight away see the hidden advantages of the situation, however small these advantages may be. This realization happens immediately and automatically, without my consciously trying to search for these advantages! In Russian, this attitude is referred to as, *"There is nothing bad without something good in it"* (нет худа без добра). Another way of putting it is, *"When bad things happen, they usually bring with them something good."* I consider this attitude to be a blessing, and I am grateful for it.

Another positive approach to life that comes naturally to me is to look at every day's life events and situations through what I refer to as my *funny glasses.* When appropriate, I may also share this observation with the people who are with me at that time. This also reminds me of a past workmate, the financial controller Colin McKenna, who used to pop into my office at the end of a long day during a difficult stage in the company's history. After discussing the events of the day, and just before leaving me, Colin used to say with his usual raspy voice and nervous chuckle, *"Whatever happens, Tom, we must never lose our sense of humour!"* He was right, of course. However, he was preaching to the converted, because I was never in any danger of losing my sense of humour. Nevertheless, I always enjoyed hearing him say it. Life would be too dull without an ever-present sense of humour! I have not seen Colin since 1975; I hope he is well and sticking to that important principle.

We should also learn to fully appreciate all of our blessings, as most of us have many that we take for granted. Unfortunately, we—myself included in the past—tend to fully appreciate our blessings only in retrospect, after we have lost them. Yet, it is never too late to start doing the right thing. I finally did, and I have felt better for it!

I had the big advantage of having been married for fifty-four years to an angel. The first twenty-two years of Lisa's life were extraordinarily hard. Hardship builds character, resilience and strength. I can say in all honesty that I always saw Lisa fully appreciating her blessings. For example, she told me that when she woke up at night, she would lie in bed literally counting, visualising and enjoying all her God-given blessings!

It is no wonder that I consider Lisa to have been my own greatest blessing in life, and even though I have not had Lisa at my side for the last five years—with her waiting for me on the other side—she will always remain my greatest blessing. Having a selfless angel as your partner and your life's true friend is a huge blessing. Thank you, dear God.

I was fortunate to meet Dr. Ken Sesel yesterday. We chatted; he sympathised with my current health problem, and I responded by saying that I am okay—that I still have many important blessings left. He thought for a while and then said to me that it was good that I am so positive. He then added, *"If only young people could be taught to fully appreciate their many blessings and to fully enjoy them starting from the time when they are still young—and never take them for granted as they grow older."*

Chapter 2

Berlin—The Lucky Escape!

The year is 2014, and my name for the last half century has been Tom Toren. For my few remaining Russian-speaking friends, my name is still Stepan or simply Styopa (*Степан Торин или просто Стёпа*).

I was born on the first of January 1931, in Berlin at the Wittenberg Platz. When I was three, my mother, who was Christian, christened me Stepan Thomas, and I was given the surname of Dr. Walter Wolffenstein who, as I mentioned earlier, was a German Jew. It seems to me that he may have wrongly assumed I was his biological son. I realized this small detail in my ancestry only much later in life, after my mother's death. This left me with no opportunity to find out who my biological father really was—that is, until I finally meet up with my mother again on the other side. By the way, my mother referred to my stepfather after the divorce as Dr. W—and so shall I. Furthermore, I shall refer to him as my stepfather, rather than my father. Another problem solved!

Four Continents/Four Cultures

In 1938, at the age of seven, fleeing from the Nazis, I was taken from Berlin through Poland, Russia, and Siberia to Harbin, a city in the north of China, not too far from the Siberian border.

At nineteen, in order to get away from Communism, I accompanied Dr. W to Israel.

On January 1, 1963 (on my thirty-second birthday), my wife, Lisa, our one-year-old daughter, Iris, and I arrived in Australia. Although we have now lived happily in Australia for fifty-one years, I shall never lose my Russian identity and my love for Russian culture.

Education

At the age of six in Berlin, I was sent to a German public Catholic school, from which I was expelled because of my stepfather's Jewish surname. At the age of seven, in Harbin, before being able to speak or understand a single word of English, I was sent to an English private school.

At the age of twelve, after the Japanese authorities forced the closure of the English school, I transferred to a Russian high school, from which I graduated at the age of seventeen at the top of my class.

At twenty-one, after completing my compulsory military service in Israel, I entered the mechanical engineering faculty of the Technion, the Israel Institute of Technology in Haifa, with no prior reading and writing knowledge of Hebrew. In spite of this serious disadvantage, and without any financial support throughout my years of study, I graduated with honours five years later. These five years were the most demanding years of my life.

My Name

My first name changed from Stepan to Tuvia and then to Tom. My wife, Lisa, and I changed our surname to Toren after we severed our relationship with the Dr. W family.

My mother was born in 1893 in Częstochowa, brought up and educated there at a time when a large part of Poland was occupied by and under the control of Russia. (See photos of my mother at the end of this chapter.) There she graduated from art school and, after the end of the First World War, married Dr. W and moved to Germany. After her divorce in 1936, she became a very well-known fashion designer in Berlin. She was Heinz Oestergaard's fashion house's principal artist before and again after the Second World War. Gusti Kaemmerling's art is still kept by the Stadt Museum of Berlin. It is quite remarkable in my opinion that, in spite of the fact that she stopped working about fifty years ago, I came across a 2011 website in which the fashion drawing selected for its front page was identified as one of hers. I kept a copy of that drawing. I am including it at the end of this chapter, together with two of her other many fashion drawings, for which I happen to have the originals.

Apart from being a leading fashion designer, my mother was also a remarkable painter in oil, watercolour, pastel, and ink. I shall come back to that later.

Unfortunately, my mother never spent much time with me or my three-years-older half-sister, Marfa/Marion; this care was delegated to our German nanny, Froli (abbreviated by me from the German word, *Frolein*), who was a very kind and dedicated elderly woman but who, needless to say, could not take the place of our absent mother.

To illustrate what I mean by "absent mother," let me recall a particular childhood experience. It happened when, as a six-year-old, I went on a school excursion boat ride along the River Spree, a narrow river with rocky banks that flows and winds through Berlin. I do not know why, but on this rare occasion, I was accompanied by my mother instead of Froli. I assume the day of the excursion coincided with the visitation day, following her divorce from Dr. W. After everyone disembarked from the boat, I lost sight of my mother. After spotting her, I ran to her and grabbed her by the hand. To my acute embarrassment, after walking with her for a few steps, the woman started laughing—it turned out not to be my mother! In retrospect, this is not surprising, considering that I cannot recall any other occasion of walking anywhere with my mother.

My mother and Dr. W were officially divorced when I reached the age of five or six. She left without saying (or rather, without *being able* to say) good-bye to Marfa and me. The day she left, we came home from the famous Berlin Zoo with Froli to find the table in Marfa's room covered with many wonderful presents. Our explanation of what had happened was left to Froli! Dr. W did not take the time to do so on that day or at any other time in the days or weeks that followed. Our mother, I assume, was not given the opportunity to do so. Strange, to say the least—don't you agree? It is fair to say that we grew up without parental love and affection. (That pink room of Marfa's and the square pink table in the centre of the room with all the presents are clearly engraved in my mind. I am sure that it is not the presents, whatever they may have been, that make me remember it so clearly!)

I was never told all the facts surrounding my mother's life and breakup with Dr. W. They were probably separated already for several years before their official divorce. Therefore, in defence of my mother, I would like to think that she may have been coerced somehow by him, to deny her any regular access to her children before the official divorce. She would have had no independent income at that stage and would have been entirely financially dependent on him until such time as she was able to establish herself in her profession as a fashion designer. Many years later, my mother told me that an enraged Dr. W used to throw empty beer bottles at her. (In fairness, I was never told the other side of that story, although, whatever it may have been, it could not justify such an action!)

This is an accurate and honest recollection of a seven-year-old boy and some retrospective interpretation of the events during that important time in my early childhood. Only after writing this chapter, editing it, and ruminating about the past did I gradually become aware of some gaps in my story and of some unexplained events. Since all of these happenings are linked together and have all occurred within a relatively short period of time, I believe I am able to fill in some of these gaps with simple, logical explanations.

Here are the important questions and answers that were bothering me.

Let me start with my first so-called "sliding-doors life event," as it would be classified by my friend and psychologist, Dr. Sarah Edelman—a strange quirk of fate whereby life may have taken us in a different direction if something had or had not happened. Staying with the "father" (which I assumed him to be at that time) was certainly not an ideal situation, but nevertheless the far better one; whereas staying with the mother and possibly being trapped in Germany during the Holocaust and the war is an absolutely horrifying thought in retrospect. Thank you, dear God, for allowing me to grow up in a Russian community in Harbin and to be brought up by two kind Russian women and to be educated in a Russian school. Thank you for that choice of sliding door and that blessing!

You will find more "sliding-door life events" in chapters 4 and 18. The second one happened when, escaping from Berlin, we were crossing the Soviet Russian and Chinese (under Japanese occupation) border.

You may have expected the verdict in the divorce-court case to assign the two children (my stepsister and me) to our mother, rather than to our father—even more so, considering that the father was Jewish. The divorce happened in 1936, and Hitler had already come to power in 1933.

Question: Why were the children awarded to the father? I thought about this many times, and one of my first answers was rather simplistic: my mother had not yet established herself in her profession; she had not yet any income of her own. Consequently, she could not support her children and was herself also still financially dependent on Dr. W's support and his alimony after the divorce. Furthermore, he quite possibly had evidence of her infidelity, which in those times was considered to be very damaging evidence in a divorce case. Dr. W would have taken full advantage of all these circumstances when negotiating the terms of settlement. He could also afford to engage the best lawyers, which my mother would not have been able to do. However, I was probably naïve in assuming that these may have been the main reasons for us staying with Dr. W. There were more compelling objectives targeted by the Nazi "justice system."

In spite of being very critical and outspoken against the church, my mother had both of us christened—me at the age of three and my half-sister at the age of six. She must have done so in order to strengthen her position in the divorce case; whereas my stepfather had me circumcised by one of his colleague doctors, as already mentioned in the introductory chapter. I do not know which came first, the christenings or the circumcision, but it certainly indicates to me that they were both competing for the children, although for different reasons.

My nanny, Froli, escorted me to and from school each day. She also took me daily to the zoo, which was my favourite place to be.

Question: Why did my mother not approach us there?

When I visited my mother in Germany thirty-five years later, she made completely unjustified critical remarks about Froli, who was a kind old woman and was good to me. Surely this was the only thing that mattered! The only explanation I can think of is that Froli would have been instructed by Dr. W to report to him if and when my mother, unbeknownst to me, tried to approach us on the street or in the zoo. This serves as supporting evidence that Dr. W was able to control my mother through her financial dependence on him. This is also the only reason I can think of to explain my mother's unfair critical remarks of Froli. Needless to say, Froli had no alternative but to follow Dr. W's instructions whilst employed by him.

The strongest indication of what had actually happened chronologically with the two court cases in 1936 is as follows.

My mother had a partner who was also Jewish, when the divorce procedings with my stepfather were initiated by her or my stepfather in or before 1936. Whilst the divorce case was still in progress, my mother and her partner were arrested by the Gestapo and charged with *Rassenschande*. These "racial-shame" trials were conducted and showcased in open courts. Punishment for "race defilement" for Jewish men was the death penalty, and for Aryan women, it was imprisonment in a concentration camp. (When Himmler asked Hitler what the punishment of women found guilty of race defilement should be, Hitler said, "Having her hair shorn off and being sent to a concentration camp.") As I mentioned earlier in this chapter, she got a lengthy prison sentence. (I do not know how long, and I was wrongly under the impression that it was prison, rather than a concentration camp.) Her partner was shot, which was the prescribed verdict after a typical "racial crime" public-exhibition trial case.

My happy fortnightly prescribed visitation days with my mother were over when she and her Jewish partner were arrested. These two to three months of fortnightly prescribed visitation days must have been a temporary arrangement by the court, subject to *the* imminent verdict in the prior racial crime public trial, with its foregone conclusion and prescribed verdict. As mentioned earlier in this chapter, I only saw my mother again for the first time twenty-two years later.

I remember an incident that must have happened around the time of the divorce. I was playing on the floor in Marfa's room, constructing something elaborate out of building blocks, when my mother briefly appeared at the door with a tall, dark man and, without saying a word to me, showed him her son and what he had built. I did not like being ignored by my mother and exhibited to a stranger. Although I was a quiet child, not prone to tantrums, this must have made me very angry, because I knocked over the building-block structure. I am only guessing, but in retrospect, I think this man must have been her lawyer. Then again, it may have been that poor man who was later executed—murdered by the Nazis! I feel very, very sorry for him and my mother.

It is amazing how certain moments in childhood stick so clearly in one's memory.

Generally speaking, it seems to me that good memories gradualy fade away over time, whilst bad memories tend to stay with us forever. This would also explain why I can remember everything in my childhood as well as I do! I wonder what my choice would be, if I were offered the ability to forget all these sad childhood memories. I think I would have to politely refuse that offer; whereas it is important to forgive whenever possible, it is equally important never to forget! We owe that to the victims.

I do not remember the apartment at the *Wittenbergplatz* because soon after I was born there, probably around 1932, we moved to an even more prestigious address at the *Kurfürstendamm 46*, corner of *Bleibtreustrasse*. This was a huge apartment, which included Dr. W's surgery and X-ray rooms. As you can see from the sketch below, the apartment had ten rooms in total, including the three bedrooms, and was elegantly furnished by my mother with antique furniture, beautiful large oil paintings, and glass vitrines with lovely porcelain figurines. I remember one living room, where the gramophone was located, furnished with light-violet silk-upholstered Biedermeier furniture, whilst the other living room with the large Blaupunkt radio had avocado-green, silk-upholstered antique Biedermeier furniture. My mother was a beautiful woman with very good, expensive taste! All this luxury was purchased with the money that Dr. W earned by selling his discovery of a venereal-disease medication to the Schering AG pharmaceutical company. The two rooms for Marfa and me were large and sunny, and the kitchen was enormous, with a huge table in the centre and several large sinks along the walls.

Although my mother obviously furnished this apartment, she must have disappeared two or three years after we moved there—certainly before I reached the age of four; otherwise I would have remembered her there.

This story would not be complete if I did not describe the strict dining regimen and discipline. Before sitting down at the dining table, we had to say the German word *Mahlzeit* (stating the obvious that it was mealtime). I had to do so until the age of twenty-four, whenever I visited my stepfather, but the meaning and significance of saying this word had never been explained to me. Before leaving the table, I had to approach my stepfather, who was sitting at the head of the table, and kiss him on his bald head and say *danke*. As a child, I was not allowed to leave anything on my plate, even though I was not given the opportunity to refuse any food I did not like before it was put on my plate. I was not a good eater in childhood, and the soup I absolutely hated was *Erbsensuppe* (pea soup). I had to keep sitting at the table for as long as it took me to finish this horrible, cooled-off soup. It took me a very long time, probably more than an hour, to finish it. To compensate for this unpleasant procedure, I was able to look at and admire the two beautiful oil paintings on the wall opposite where I was sitting (as shown in the apartment sketch). The larger of the two paintings, about 1.2 metres by 0.9 metres, had tall, leafy trees in the left foreground and a country road crossing fields diagonally across the painting, all the way to the horizon. The somewhat smaller painting was equally beautiful, with a similar paysage. Needless to say, being seven years old or younger, I had no idea who the artist was, whereas now in retrospect, knowing my mother's expensive taste, it would have undoubtedly been by a well-known top artist.

As mentioned earlier, after the divorce, Froli started bringing Marfa and me to visit our mother every fortnight. At that stage, she lived in a single room plus studio apartment in Dahlem, Berlin, once again tastefully furnished and decorated. (See photo.) These visits were truly quality time I was able to spend with her! I used to sit next to her or on her knees at her large, brightly illuminated horizontal drawing board, whilst she was making exquisite drawings of different animals for me, quickly finishing them in watercolours as only she could. Her watercolour technique for animal fur and feathers was amazing. We still have some of her small watercolour paintings of animals. Sometimes I watched her making fashion drawings. These are the memories of my mother that I treasure. I think, considering how little time I was able to spend with my mother before her divorce, these would have been the best hours of my entire childhood.

A few months later, she was gone—arrested and imprisoned by the Nazis for *Rassenschande*, the racial shame of living with a Jew. Her partner, after the breakup with Dr. W, was also Jewish. As I have learned since, the Jewish male partners who committed this "crime" did not go to jail—they were executed. This was the prescribed verdict. Christian women were normally imprisoned but not executed.

To one of my birthdays, my mother gave me the present of a light-green budgie, whose given name was Joko. I do not know how she managed to give or send me that present, because she was already a *persona non-grata* (a person who is no longer welcome) in Dr.W's home. My stepfather was raving mad, saying that budgies are carriers of TB. So Joko was kept in the living room where the Blaupunkt radio was located, instead of my bedroom. Joko was looked after by our cook. She was born in the South of Germany and when she taught Joko to speak, he adopted her accent and intonation of speech, with emphasis on the first syllable saying:"*Joko, willst du baden gehen?*" (Joko, would you like to take a bath?)

When I went with Froli to the zoo, I sketched many of the animals. In spite of my tender age, I took my hobby very seriously. My childhood dream was to travel to Africa and become a zoologist. Throughout my life, I have been fascinated by animals and nature in all its forms.

My boyhood friend in Harbin, Kolya Peshkovsky, was given a present by his father of two thick volumes of *The Life of Animals.* These famous books by the German scientist Alfred Brehm—translated into Russian, with detailed descriptions of animals, their habitat, and life, with beautiful ink illustrations—became my favourite books.

Nowadays, instead of watching animals in the Kalahari, I watch with absolute fascination and awe when unbelievably tiny insects and spiders, about two millimetres long, run at high speed across my desk. Using my seven-times printer's magnifying glass, I observe their little faces and feet with perfectly formed joints that enable them to achieve a *running speed vs. body mass* that is two thousand times greater than that of humans. Here is my calculation: the wee insect's weight may reach, say, 70 mg, which would make us at, say, 70 kg, 1 million times greater in mass—and yet, these tiny insects run across my desk at a speed of one metre per minute, which *pro rata to mass* would require us to run 1 million m/min = 1,000 km per minute = 60,000 km per hour. How about that! And yet, we take these little miracles of creation and evolution in nature that surround us for granted. (Please bear in mind that I only made these speeds proportional to our relative body masses, which may be an inadequate comparison, but an interesting comparison nevertheless. As we know, these little insects and we, humans, had a common ancestor.)

Let me share with you my interpretation of another little miracle of nature. I am thinking of Darwin's grand idea of evolution by natural selection as it applies to the creation of all the beautiful flowers that we admire and enjoy. They evolved over millions of years to become more and more beautiful—not to attract us humans, but to compete in their ability to attract the insects that pollinate them. So, who are the true judges of flowers' beauty, if not insects? Nevertheless, I have never read or heard of anyone crediting insects for their good taste.

Thirty-nine years ago, our daughter, Iris, at the age of fourteen, became a vegetarian overnight, after she was challenged by one of her high school teachers, who asked her, "If you love animals, why do you eat them?" Her mother, Lisa, followed Iris's lead straight away. I followed their lead several months later. (I have always been a bit slow!) Twenty-one-year-old Laura has never tasted meat since her birth. Unfortunately, we are all born and brought up in a society in which killing other animals and eating their flesh is accepted as normal, even though we evolved without claws and sharp teeth for tearing the prey apart. Our very long intestines, typical for all other herbivorous animals, did not evolve for the digestion of flesh, typical for all carnivorous animals.

With the world's population growing from 1 billion in 1800 to 7 billion in 2011, the meat industry introduced factory farming to satisfy the rapidly growing market demand. As a result, contrary to earlier centuries, animals are now required to live miserable, short lives in dark, confined, or overcrowded spaces on concrete floors or in wire cages before they are killed for the meat industry for human consumption. I doubt whether religious leaders—some of whom sanctioned the eating of meat during the early centuries— would have sanctioned factory farming as practiced in the twentieth and twenty-first centuries. Sir Paul McCartney has been quoted as saying, *"If slaughterhouses had glass walls, everyone would be a vegetarian."*

Allow me to share one more thought with you on the subject of animal-rights, namely, the inadequancy of the frequently expressed concern about the preservation of species for the benefit of our children and *future generations* being able to see them. This concern is inadequate because the *future generations* of those animals do not get a mention in these comments. Furthermore, I feel that the peaceful survival of *individual animals* without fear and suffering, rather than the species as a whole, is of paramount importance. In brief, I believe we do not have the right to subject animals to cruelty and suffering.

Sometimes, Froli and I walked in the *Tiergarten*, which translates to "animal garden." This is a very large natural park, very good for walking, close to the centre of Berlin. It used to be a recreational park for German nobility a few centuries ago, where they indulged in the "sport" of hunting deer—not much of a sport and certainly not an animal garden for the deer!

A happy time of my early childhood was when my stepfather drove us in his grey Opel to the farm, Guthaus Blau, near a small place called Menz, north of Berlin. There I could spend time in the beautiful, pristine pine forest, looking for and watching the forest animals. To be able to enjoy the ambience of European pine forests with their beautiful, rich undergrowth, the forest animals, and unique gentle sounds of birds became my lifelong obsession, one that was never properly fulfilled. Unfortunately, there are no such forests around Sydney, and most of the forests we visited during our trips to Europe in the last forty-plus years have been a disappointment because of their partial destruction by acid rain. One notable happy exception was a small section of forest that we explored in St. Moritz, Switzerland. When we tried to find it again a few years later, it seemed to have vanished.

During one of my business trips, I happened to be in Zurich on a weekend. So naturally, true to my earlier-mentioned obsession, I was keen to spend some time in a beautiful forest. I joined a tourist bus to drive across the border to the Black Forest, with the expectation of spending some quality time in that famous forest. It was a rather long drive. When we reached our destination, the bus stopped in front of a souvenir shop. The tourist guide announced that we had to be back within twenty minutes. The passengers rushed to the souvenir shop, whilst I ran ahead along the road to an entrance to the forest. The tall pine trees had succumbed to acid rain, with their yellowish-grey dead needles covering the ground; there was no undergrowth—end of story. I returned to the bus in time for our journey back to the hotel.

As is customary in Germany, at the age of six, I was sent to a public school for boys, with a very large, colourful paper cone-shaped *Tüte* filled with various sweets. It was an old, gloomy building with dark classrooms and an inner courtyard paved with large cobblestones—all very depressing! I do not think I ever complained about it, but every morning, as Froli was escorting me to school, I had to stop halfway to school at one particular small tree and vomit up my breakfast. I did not stay in this school for very long—I was expelled because of my stepfather's Jewish surname. I then attended a private school for boys and girls. I think it was called *Schelschule* (or something like it) but, once again, I was only there for a few months. This school was much brighter and had a friendlier environment.

I can remember and visualise two school experiences. One happened in the gloomy inner courtyard of the public school, where a rather large bully started hitting a much smaller boy. I stood up for the little fellow, and the bully backed off. As they say, self-praise is no recommendation, but I truly believe that from that first experience and for the rest of my life, I could never witness injustice without getting involved and fighting against it. I always stood up and fought for the people I could help, especially those people with whom I worked and for whom I was responsible. I resigned twice in Israel from senior positions of chief engineer, in protest against the unfair treatment of employees. In doing so, I brought about the dismissal of the general managers to whom I was responsible at that time. (More about this later.)

The second really frightening experience happened in the brightly lit, large assembly hall of the private school, when the whole school was gathered and singing the German hymn, "*Deutschland, Deutschland über alles, über alles in der Welt*" (Germany, Germany above everything, above everything in the world). I stood there, a very frightened six-year-old boy, knowing that I was expected to sing, but not singing. This song was followed by the *Horst Wessel* march "*SA marschiert, die Reihen fest geschlossen!*" (SA is marching in closed ranks!)—Once again, I stood there without singing. Shortly after that, I was again expelled.

One day, when I was six years old, I was walking home with my stepfather, when we were approached by a uniformed member of the Hitler Youth or the SA, asking for a Winter Appeal donation. My stepfather kept walking and responded by saying that he only donates to the Jewish Winter Appeal. The enraged Nazi blocked our way, confronted us, and screamed at the top of his voice, *"Du Jüdischer Schweinehund!"* (You Jewish swine-dog!), to which I cheekily replied *"Wer es sagt, ist es selber,"* (Whoever says it, is it himself). This was a popular saying amongst children at play. The Nazi did not expect this; he stepped aside and let us proceed on our way. He may have been a young, misguided Nazi who retained deep down some remnant of decency and who loved children, especially blond children like me.

I also remember the *Kristallnacht* pogrom, the Night of Broken Glass, when a huge Nazi crowd was advancing slowly in the western direction along the *Kurfürstendamm* from the *Kaiser-Wilhelm-Gedächtnis-Kirche* (*Memorial Church*) towards our building on the corner of *Bleibtreustrasse*. As the menacing mob was moving closer, Dr. W had the presence of mind to rush downstairs and unscrew and remove the yellow doctor's sign. The yellow sign was compulsory to inform the public that the practicing doctor was a Jew. Had he not done so, things would have turned out very differently, and you would not be reading my life story now, because we would not have been able to leave Germany soon after that pogrom.

This violent *Kristallnacht* pogrom broke out all over Germany and Austria on November 9, 1938 and lasted for two days. Members of the SS, SA (Sturmabteilung), Hitler Youth, and ordinary citizens smashed Jewish shop windows (hence the name *Kristallnacht),* broke into and looted Jewish businesses and private homes, beating up and murdering Jews; they destroyed and burned down Jewish schools and synagogues, desecrating sacred Torah scrolls. The police and fire brigades stood by but did not interfere with the mob's murderous and destructive actions. You will find more information and many photos on the Internet.

A few days following this two-day-long pogrom, I remember walking with Froli along the streets of our neighbourhood and seeing all the broken shop windows and ransacked shops, including the demolished small shop of a friendly cobbler whom I liked to visit and chat with. I also remember the large stars of David painted on many walls and remaining shop windows, and the burned-down synagogue on the *Fasanenstrasse* with a huge pile of burned, smouldering books in front of it.

About a week later, we left Berlin for Harbin, China. As we were leaving, my mother was still in prison. I did not see my mother until twenty-two years later in the UK.

Standing at the window of the train carriage, I cried bitterly, saying good-bye to Froli on the platform below. Froli cried too, whilst Marfa was running back and forth though the corridor of the carriage, excited about the long journey ahead.

We were amongst the lucky ones who managed to escape from hell.

BERLIN 1931-1938

21

Oberhof-1937

Harbin-1942

1950: Abendkleid mit Tüllstola, gezeichnet von
Gusti Kämmerling

My mum as a child and teenager
in Czestochowa

Gusti Kämmerling 1959

Gusti Kämmerling 1960, Berlin teenagers

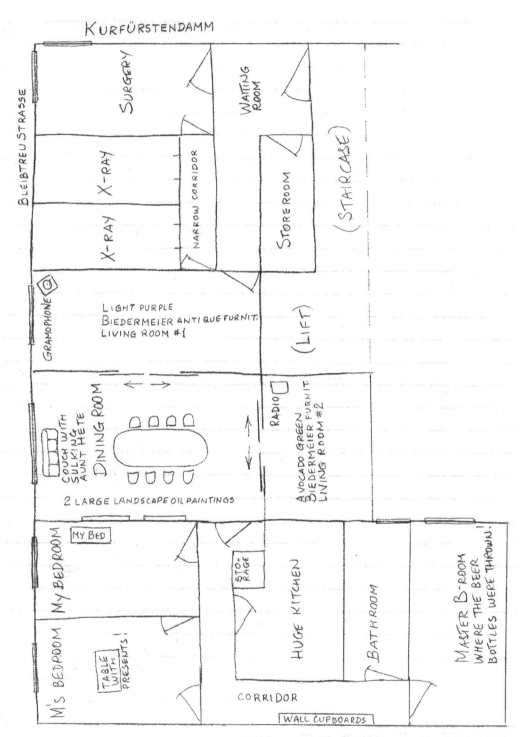

KURFÜRSTENDAMM

BLEIBTREU STRASSE

SURGERY

X-RAY

X-RAY

X-RAY

NARROW CORRIDOR

WAITING ROOM

STORE ROOM

(STAIRCASE)

GRAMOPHONE

LIGHT PURPLE
BIEDERMEIER ANTIQUE FURNIT.
LIVING ROOM #1

(LIFT)

DINING ROOM

COUCH WITH
SULKING AUNT HETE

RADIO

AVOCADO GREEN
BIEDERMEIER FURNIT.
LIVING ROOM #2

2 LARGE LANDSCAPE OIL PAINTINGS

MY BEDROOM

MY BED

M'S BEDROOM

TABLE WITH PRESENTS!

STO-RAGE

HUGE KITCHEN

BATHROOM

MASTER B-ROOM
WHERE THE BEER
BOTTLES WERE THROWN!

CORRIDOR

WALL CUPBOARDS

Our home at Kurfürstendamm 46, B E R L I N

Chapter 3

Sad Reflections—Trying to Comprehend!

One of Dr. W's three brothers, Albert Wolffenstein, was a distinguished architect with many prominent buildings to his credit. He was the only member of the large Wolffenstein family in Berlin who survived the Holocaust. Whilst he was preparing firewood, a wooden splinter lodged in his eye. Being a Jew, he was denied treatment in hospital. Consequently, he lost sight in that eye. This must have happened shortly before the outbreak of war. He died soon after the end of World War II. I used to visit his wife, Toni, whenever I was in Germany on business. She was Christian. She gave me a large, heavy book for safekeeping, containing very impressive photos and drawings of many of his architectural creations. Dr. W's other two brothers and one sister, Hethe, and their families perished in the Holocaust. Hethe's only daughter managed to flee to New York, where she eventually committed suicide. Another brother of Dr. W also committed suicide. I do not know any further details about that brother or any other relatives.

Here are some simple, awful statistics that I learned a few years ago, after watching the film *Judgment at Nuremberg* with Spencer Tracy:

On the tragic day of 9/11 in 2001, almost three thousand innocent people perished in New York, with their loved ones left suffering their loss since then and into the future. Man's inhumanity is limitless!

During the five and a half years from late 1939 till mid-1945, i.e., over approximately two thousand days, the Nazis murdered 6 million Jews. This means that, *on average, the same number of* three thousand *innocent people were murdered every day for each of these two thousand days*. This does not include the 2.5 million gentile Poles and hundreds of thousands of Romanies, homosexuals, physically ill and mentally retarded people, political opponents, and others.

For Russia, Ukraine, and the rest of the fifteen Soviet republics, the Second World War lasted from June 22, 1941 to May 9, 1945 which equals approximately 1,420 days. About 25 million people perished in the Soviet Union during that time, with *more than half of that number being civilian deaths, i.e., an average of 17,600 soldiers and civilians dying every day for each of these 1,420 days.*

The human mind struggles to comprehend large figures. I am unable to visualize a crowd of, say, 1 million people, i.e., a crowd of one thousand thousands—this seems to be beyond me! This is why I felt that these *daily figures* of 3,000 and 17,600 would help me to comprehend the magnitude of what happened in those years of brutality and murder.

Having done the cold maths of millions, I then tried to think of the *individual victims,* their fear and suffering for their loved ones and themselves whilst anticipating their families' and their own inevitable demise. We can only try to imagine the fear and suffering that preceded those deaths. It seems to me that this fear and anticipation of death must have been far worse than the moment of death itself.

Future generations should be informed about the Holocaust and all other genocides in Asia and Africa of the twentieth century. Children should be taught in ethics classes about empathy and compassion for humans and all other life on Earth.

Chapter 4

Berlin–Warsaw–Moscow–Irkutsk–Harbin—The First Long Journey

Prior to our departure for Harbin, Dr. W had been waiting for our visas to Argentina, which were promised to him by one of his patients, the Argentine consul in Berlin. The visas never eventuated. When it became critically urgent to leave Germany and Dr. W asked the consul for the granting of our visa applications to be expedited, he was told by the consul that our visa applications were no longer active, because my mother had informed him some years ago that our plans to move to Argentina had been superseded. This illustrates the friendly relationship and close communication that prevailed between my mother and Dr. W before and after their separation, even in such extreme matters as survival.

Dr. W. had taken up a relationship with a Russian woman, one of my mother's acquaintances. Through that woman, he made contact with a Russian doctor in Harbin, China, Dr. Stasya Basina, who was prepared to sponsor us, with the view of establishing a joint medical practice with Dr. W. On the strength of that sponsorship, a visa application was lodged with the Japanese consulate, because the Japanese Imperial Army had occupied Manchuria in 1932. As far as I know, we had no alternative but to leave Berlin before the visas were formally granted.

And so, after the tearful good-byes with Froli, the train left Berlin, and within about a day or two, having safely crossed the German border into Poland, we reached its capital, Warsaw. This was the first highlight of the journey, because a family friend brought us some wonderful Polish dark- and light-coloured halva to the train. This was the first time that we had tasted the rich, sweet taste of halva—it was delicious!

The second and main highlight was the stopover in Moscow. That was really exciting. Naturally, I did not know at the age of seven what I was looking at, but nevertheless, Moscow in general and the Kremlin domes in particular were very impressive and colourful. The underground Metro stations were also beautiful, with their marble walls. However, travelling in the extremely overcrowded Metro trains, standing-room only and being squeezed between all the big adults, was a bit scary. I also remember the very spacious restaurant with tiled floor and a big, round pool with large carp swimming in it, unaware that the next guest may select any one of them for dinner.

The Trans-Siberian Railway, stretching for about ten thousand kilometres, is by far the longest rail line in the world—about twice as long as the one between the East and West Coast of the United States. Our compartment was comfortable. We were even able to order some black caviar; however, it did not make much of an impression on me. The journey across the Ural Mountains and all the way to Irkutsk took many days, with very little to see because the windows were frozen over most of the time. We did, however, get a glimpse of the famous Lake Baikal in the far distance. It is the largest and deepest lake in the world and is fed by several hundred rivers. Lake Baikal holds 20 percent of the Earth's fresh water. It is home to countless species of plants and animals. It would, no doubt, have been extremely interesting for me as a grown-up to visit and explore—but life is too short.

When we got off the train in Irkutsk, the temperature was minus 63 degrees centigrade (or minus 81 degrees Fahrenheit). I guess it must have been a cold day—don't you think? I have both heard and read that some birds freeze in flight and drop dead to the ground in such cold. Fortunately, I have never witnessed this in Harbin, which also has a Siberian climate, but naturally, these extremely cold days are the exception. In fact, I was told that the year after we left Harbin, the temperature dropped to minus 68 degrees centigrade, and many farm animals perished.

The explanation for birds freezing to death in flight, I believe, is that the faster the birds fly, the firmer their feathers are being pressed against their little bodies by the surrounding airstream pressure, thereby depriving them of the heat-insulating effect of the warmer air trapped between their feathers.

Even though we had no scientific weather forecasts in those days, my friend Kolya and I occasionally used to travel by train beyond the outskirts of Harbin in the middle of winter and walk for a whole day through the open countryside. The object of these excursions was to shoot pheasants. Fortunately, I was a poor shot, and the pheasants were in no danger from me. However, this did not diminish the wickedness of my intensions. I was young and ignorant, with no parents or role model to guide me.

Our toes are the Achilles' heel in those super-freezing temperatures, so we wore oversize boots to accommodate two pairs of very thick woollen socks, wrapped in newspaper to trap the insulating warm air.

Back to our trans-Siberian voyage in 1938. I found it very cosy, falling asleep to the regular clicking noise of the train's wheels as they rolled across the small expansion gaps between one rail and the next. Many years later, when travelling in Europe with Lisa, Iris, and Laura, these clicking noises no longer had the same effect of enhancing my sleep. The difference, I assume, was in my age—not in the wheels.

It took us somewhat longer than the usual seven to ten days to travel through Siberia. When the train stopped at the Manchurian border, I recall the rather small border-control post building with several Japanese officials who conducted all their questioning in an aggressive, shouting fashion, the way it is sometimes portrayed in films. We did not have official visas, and the documents we did have did not satisfy them. Our problem was that we could no longer delay our departure from Berlin whilst waiting for our visas to be issued by the Japanese Consulate.

We arrived at another "sliding doors" situation, except this time, the choice of preferred door was certainly not ours to make. It was entirely up to the guards. In retrospect, I guess, our chances at that point of entering China must have been less than 10 percent.

Yet, minutes before the train's departure, the unfriendly guards pointed at the train and angrily shouted to us to get on board. Actions always speak louder than words! May God bless their souls for their compassion. Our documents were stamped just a few minutes before the train's last departure whistle, after we were allowed to board. It must have been extremely stressful for my stepfather.

Without the guards disobeying their instructions, we would have had only one alternative: to return to Germany, where we no longer had a home and where we would have been accommodated in one of the concentration camps.

Sure, our lives hung by a thread, but we were lucky, thanks to the Japanese border control officers' unexpected compassion. Our suffering was nothing compared to the suffering in 2014 of Middle Eastern and African asylum-seekers during their long, perilous journeys to Australia, which ends with fifteen to twenty days and nights in leaky, unseaworthy boats on their last leg from Indonesia to Australia. Can you imagine the despair of these people when their boats are being turned around for yet another fifteen to twenty days' and nights' horrific return trip—the only difference being that, when they arrive back in Indonesia, they will have already spent all their savings and they may have also put their relatives back home into serious debt.

I especially think of the poor, suffering, seasick women having to care for their babies without proper toilets, without proper washing facilities, without diapers, and without medical care. So much for our government's plan of "turning the boats around." Shame, Australia, shame! We could and should definitely be able to do better than that. In fact, it is our international obligation to do so.

So, full credit to the Japanese border control people who, in spite of their unfriendly behaviour towards us, understood our desperate situation and allowed us to proceed on our journey. People should be judged by their actions, rather than by what they say and whether they behave in a friendly manner or not. I can only imagine that their instructions would have been simple and straightforward: let those who have visas pass; turn those who have no visas back. Simple!

Speaking of asylum, let me say that our Australian politicians use the poor, wretched asylum-seekers from the Middle East and Asia who arrive in their unseaworthy boats on our shores for their own political and personal objectives to be elected or reelected, whatever the case may be. The politicians demonise the asylum-seekers and use them for political point-scoring in their parliamentary debates on immigration and to demonstrate their toughness to the electorate, especially when campaigning prior to elections. Instead, they should finally agree to deal with this divisive issue in a *bipartisan,* constructive, and compassionate manner. It seems to me that most of these politicians lack life experience. They grew up without experiencing any hardships and persecution dangers, and they lack the imagination to develop any empathy with the asylum-seekers—and without empathy, there cannot be any meaningful compassion. This is very sad, very sad indeed!

Instead of denying asylum-seekers the help they deserve and are entitled to under international law, we should be preparing for more asylum-seekers in the years to come as sea levels rise and inhabitants of some of our surrounding island nations will be forced to abandon their gradually disappearing island homes.

Sadly, it also seems to me that, hypothetically speaking, if these asylum-seekers were to come here from the British Isles or at least from the European continent, as a result of some natural disaster, their accommodation in Australia would not present any problems. Racism is ugly and cruel, as well as extremely stupid, because it does not make any sense whatsoever. Mental capacities of individuals, their intelligence, kindness, empathy, and compassion, are not influenced by their ethnicity. Unfortunately, individuals' racist prejudices are mostly influenced during childhood by their parents and family environment. Trying to be positive, I am hoping that global communication and the Internet are bringing all of us closer together and will eventually defeat global racism.

In the meantime, we should lobby our politicians, urging them to take positive action whenever and wherever racism raises its ugly head. Think of the saying, *"All that is required for evil to succeed is for good people to do nothing."*

Chapter 5

Harbin—A Big Improvement in My Life

I cannot remember arriving at Harbin's Central Railway Station. I must have been asleep at the time. I also have no recollection of arriving at our new home at 47 Birgevaya Street in the Pristajn District of the city.

The entirely different new life, the different surroundings, being away from the isolated life with no friends, both grown-ups and children, that my stepfather created for us in Berlin, and most importantly, being amongst Russian people and Russian culture became a very positive change in my life. However, it must have been a culture shock for my German stepfather. This also proved to be an important factor in estranging me from him as years went by.

Russia played a major part in Harbin's history. From what I learned whilst growing up there, Harbin was still a Chinese fishing village on the banks of the Songhua River for most of the nineteenth century. (We called it Sungari, meaning "White River" in an old Chinese dialect.) I was told that Harbin was transformed into a railway town by Russian engineers in 1897 when Russia commenced building the Trans-Manchurian Railway. Then, starting in 1917, white Russians fleeing the red Bolshevik Revolution emigrated to Harbin, thereby creating the largest Russian community outside Russia, which reached a population of 120,000 in Harbin alone and another 35,000 in surrounding railway townships. In 1932, the Japanese Imperial Army occupied Harbin and the rest of Manchuria, which they renamed Manchukuo until, in 1945, the Soviet Red Army "liberated" us by driving the Japanese army out and evacuating the Japanese civilian population back to Japan. In 1949, Stalin turned Harbin over to Mao Tse-tung and the People's Republic of China.

Harbin is the capital of the Heilongjiang Province in northeastern China and is now a major industrial, cultural, and educational centre. Harbin was referred to as both the "Oriental St. Petersburg" and the "Oriental Moscow" because of last century's Russian-influenced architecture. Harbin is a favourite Russian tourist centre, and the second language is once again becoming Russian.

Unfortunately, Harbin is also known for its experimental Unit 73, located somewhere outside the city, where the Japanese were developing and testing chemical and bacteriological weapons during World War II, using Chinese, Russian, and Allied prisoners.

You may be interested to look at some of the many Harbin websites about its amazing history of development as a Russian cultural centre in the first half of the twentieth century, and its development in the second half of the twentieth century as a Chinese cultural and industrial centre, with the Harbin University of Science and Technology (HUST), the Harbin Medical University, many Russian students, and flourishing tourism. Also look at photos of the old Russian churches, some of which were destroyed during the Cultural Revolution, and of course, photos of Harbin's world-famous magnificent ice sculptures on the frozen Songhua River. These ice sculptures are very artistic and beautiful. To create any one of them would have taken many weeks of work in the open, windy, freezing cold, wearing heavy clothing and thick gloves. Not easy! Only in China! I spent much of my childhood—in summer in the water and in winter on the metre-thick ice of the wide, beautiful Sungari River.

And so, forward into the past. I arrived into a different, better world. I shall start by describing my physical surroundings, and then I shall try to fit into it all the new people in my life.

Birgevaya Street was a wide crossroad of the main street, Kitayskaya. This 1.5-kilometre-long main street ended at the beautiful Sungari River promenade. Like most of the roads, Birgevaya was cobblestone-paved. Our Number 47 was a two-storey brick building that was built by Dr. Basina's parents who, I was told, made some of their money through the opium trade. In the middle of the building's façade was a large, arched, wrought-iron gate, the type you would find in Russia or in Paris. This gate led to a very large courtyard. At the back of the courtyard were two adjacent single-storey wooden buildings, occupied by two Japanese families, Kumita San and Chiginaga San— one of them Buddhist and the other Shinto. I liked listening to the repetitive, rhythmic sound of their prayer sticks. I have never heard of any ethnic tensions between these two religions. There is, however, racial discrimination against Koreans living in Japan.

The spacious arched passage beneath the main building, leading from the arched gate to the courtyard, was occupied by a family of swallows that had built their clay nest by attaching it to the centre of the arched ceiling. I do not know which religion they belonged to, but they came back religiously every spring and departed to warmer climates in autumn. I loved watching them in flight and looked forward to their arrival every spring.

In the years to follow, I often played with Chieko San, the sweet little daughter of the Chiginaga San family. I also had private lessons with Mrs. Ono and spoke Japanese quite well, writing in Katakana and Hiragana alphabets and a few Japanese and Chinese characters. Mrs. Ono San was a hunchbacked, elderly Russian lady who was married to a Japanese man—hence the name Ono. She and her husband, Mr. Ono San, had one large room in their home that was occupied solely by canary and ricebirds— unfortunately, all in cages.

I also had private Chinese lessons with Mr. Wong, who used to say "woh" ("I" in Chinese) whilst pointing at the tip of his nose with his long-nailed pointer finger. Can you imagine—living in China and being surrounded by Chinese culture, we were not taught Mandarin at either the English primary school or the Russian high school? It could not have been anything other than the deeply rooted racism and a lack of respect for other nationalities and their cultures by our "superior" older generation. We, the children, were the obvious losers. Not being able to speak Mandarin now is one of my serious regrets in life.

We lived on the second floor. The sunny bedroom I shared with Marfa looked out on Birgevaya Street. It had a small balcony where I kept my tortoise and lizards in summer and where we grew red geraniums in flower boxes and special ivy with lovely, bell-shaped blue flowers, called *viewny* in Russian. Our bedroom consisted of a mismatch of various furniture styles and colours: two very different beds, one polished-brass bed for me and the other a large, wooden one, painted light-beige for Marfa; a small, semicircular, light-green table with three carved legs at the foot end of her bed; some pink shelving; a grey cupboard; Marfa's beautiful antique lacquered desk; my very old, small school desk with integral seat, which many years prior to its occupation by me used to be white; and an old but beautiful piano. The window and balcony's glass door were fitted with glass shelving for various small plants and cacti. Soon after we occupied the room, the old, worn wooden floor was covered with plain, brown linoleum (vinyl). The very high, heavy, solid timber door was fitted with huge brass handles.

The double windows, with about one hundred millimetres (four inches) of space between them, were both sealed each autumn for the duration of winter, with only a small rectangular window (*fortochka*) in the top-right corner of each window for daily airing of the room. The freezing-cold air streaming into the room through those little top windows would condense instantly and drop to floor level in a continuous serpentlike stream. Both the external and internal windows were sealed with a special homemade putty (*samaska*), glued over with strips of white paper. Cotton wool was placed at the bottom, between the two windows. The temperature outside sometimes dropped at night to minus 40 degrees centigrade and below. A large wood-and-coal-fired stove, tiled all the way from the floor to the high ceiling, was located inside the wall opposite the window, next to the door, serving both our room and the adjacent room.

The adjacent large dining room was dark and furnished with Stasya Basina's very heavy, old-fashioned black-lacquered furniture, some of it with mirrors, along two opposite walls. I may have seen uglier furniture at some time during my long life, but I certainly cannot remember when and where. I am sure Alfred Hitchcock could have put it to good use. Oh yes, there was also a very large grandfather clock (colour—you guessed it—black) with several large, heavy brass descending weights that had to be wound up once a week. It chimed in increasing lengths of time at each quarter, half, three-quarter, and full hours, day and night. Another good one for Mr. Hitchcock! A few months later, when three large crates with Dr. W's X-ray and other medical equipment arrived, some of my mother's chosen antique Biedermeier furniture arrived with it. This furniture was sprinkled tastefully amongst the grotesque black funeral-parlour furniture, providing an interesting contrast. In the middle of this cheerful dining room was a very long and wide black-lacquered table with matching ugly black chairs with black leather upholstery. Sitting in that large room by yourself could really uplift your spirits!

I have provided a sketch of the apartment to help you visualise its layout and feel its atmosphere. (Don't forget to turn on the light!)

Past the dining room were the servants' quarters, the toilet, bathroom, kitchen, and exit to the rear staircase, as well as a small two-room apartment, where Stasya Basina accommodated her mentally disturbed brother, Lyova, and her nutty old aunt, Basya, who was supposed to look after Lyova. From time to time, Stasya and Basya got into shouting and cursing matches. I never took the trouble to listen and find out what it was all about. Now I'll never know what I may have missed! So be it. What an interesting family! More about all this later.

Naturally, there were no electrical or gas hot plates and stoves, refrigerators or dishwashers in those days. Food was prepared on a large brick stove with a cast-iron top and in an integral oven—all fired by wood and coal. Also, believe it or not, there were no computers, mobile phones, TVs, transistor radios, traffic lights, plastic packaging, and days off on Saturday. All this was invented later.

Coming back to the kitchen: all fruit and vegetables had to be rinsed at all times in a strong solution of dark-purple disinfecting crystals of potassium permanganate ($KMnO4$), because of the endemic typhoid.

I shall save you the monotony of reading the description of the other four rooms in our apartment, except to say that one was occupied by Dr. W, another one by the owner, Dr. Basina, and the remaining two were converted into surgery rooms, with one of them housing the X-ray diagnostic and treatment equipment, as well as diathermy equipment, etc. (I forgot to mention earlier that Dr. W specialized in skin and venereal diseases, including X-ray diagnostics and therapy.) All that X-ray equipment was installed and maintained by a very clever Italian technician, Sr. Penko, who also looked after our illegal shortwave Blaupunkt radio. The radio was eventually confiscated by the Japanese not-so-secret police, who raided our home in the middle of the night, searching for incriminating, subversive information, and arresting Dr. Basina on suspicion of spying for the Soviet Union. She spent about half a year in jail, where she was tortured by being hung by her limbs from the ceiling, and where she contracted typhus. The suspicion of spying was probably based on the fact that she had a kept man (*soopnik*), Valdemar, who was a Soviet citizen (but who did not believe in the virtues of work).

So, now that you can picture our habitat, I shall do my best to describe some of the other inhabitants, starting with Dr. W.

As mentioned earlier, only after my mother had already passed away in 1978 did I realize that Dr. W could not have been my biological father, whereas Marfa, being three years older than me, was indeed his biological daughter and my half-sister. There was also a strong facial resemblance between Marfa and Dr. W. I should have suspected and realised all this much earlier because, thank God, I had absolutely nothing in common with him and her, both physically and character-wise. Besides, by the time I was conceived, the relationship between him and my mother had already deteriorated to the point where she could no longer spend any time at our home. This would also explain why I referred to her in chapter two as the "absent mother."

When I finally realized that Dr. W was not my biological father, I was very pleased, because during my adolescence, I liked him less and less—not only for what he did to me or did not do for me, but for the type of person he was. Judging by what I kept overhearing during his discussions with Dr. Basina at the dinner table, he had very little compassion and consideration for his poorer Chinese patients. His demands from the servants were also unreasonable and inconsiderate. For example, he forbade the Russian maid, Lisa, to use the normal laundry board, demanding that she wash all our laundry by hand in the bathtub. The poor woman complained bitterly but had no alternative but to follow his instruction. In addition, his interaction with most people was too judgemental and disrespectful, in my opinion. He was on bad terms with all his medical colleagues, of whom there were many in Harbin amongst the German Jews.

With regard to what he did to me or did not do for me during my childhood, I believe that generally speaking, as children, we accept everything as being normal. Only as adults, with the benefit of some acquired wisdom, are we capable of considering the past with deeper understanding and objectivity.

Dr. W was born in 1885, making him fifty-three by the time we arrived in Harbin. He was somewhat below average height, stocky, almost bald, with bulging eyes, a fleshy nose, low cheekbones, tobacco-stained small teeth, an unhealthy colour of skin, and large hands with the shortest, thickest fingers I have ever seen. Credit where credit is due, he did provide well financially for my half-sister and me. However, I received no other support and no guidance from him whatsoever. He seldom spoke, and when he did, it was by way of giving me instructions on what to do or not to do. He also liked to dish out heavy-handed Prussian physical punishment. After hitting me across the face, he asked me why I looked at him with such hatred!

He mellowed with age and poor health in his seventies in Israel, and I was kind and considerate to him until the time I severed my relationship with Marfa, him, and Stasya. I will go into detail about that and specifically about Marfa's betrayal of me and my wife, Lisa, in one of the following chapters. In a nutshell, as you can see, it was a dysfunctional family, but you have heard nothing yet.

Another small detail: my stepfather never spoke to me about his childhood, his parents, his school and university years, or his many siblings (even after finding out that they had perished in the Holocaust). He never mentioned his work, his invention, his marriage to my mother, except for saying once that during their honeymoon, they were in Venice on the Piazza San Marco, but that was in response to a question about a photograph. I cannot remember him ever speaking to me or asking me about my school, my homework, my teachers, my school friends, my piano-playing progress, my soccer playing, my interest or lack thereof in the opposite sex, my work at the factory, or my depressed mood at the age of seventeen and eighteen. When comparing my loveless childhood to that of our daughter, Iris, and granddaughter, Laura, my early life seems bizarre! This is one reason why in the introduction, I said that writing my life story has been a cathartic experience for me. There is more in this chapter and in the chapters that follow.

Growing up without a mother did not seem to cause me any serious heartache during my childhood and teenage years, simply because I did not know what I was missing. In retrospect, I now realize clearly what I have missed and how that affected my childhood and my development as a child and teenager. I enjoy seeing the loving relationship between Iris and Laura. At every opportunity now, I love watching the beautiful interaction between mothers and their children—when I am sitting in a doctor's waiting room, in an airport lounge, in a restaurant, travelling by train, etc. I am happy when I see this, but it also makes me a little sad about what I missed.

My first governess after we arrived in Harbin was Aleksandra Vakulovna, a rather strict but fair-minded lady. Although she was not very affectionate to me, I cried bitterly to stop her when she threatened to leave me for good because I had been naughty. I am not sure why I cried so bitterly. I can only imagine that having been left by my mother and then losing Froli, I got a bit desperate at the thought that I may lose Aleksandra Vakulovna as well. After all, I was only seven years old and needed someone to love me.

Eventually, Aleksandra Vakulovna did leave me, and her place was taken by Lidia Ivanovna Zakrjevskaya (her late husband's Polish surname). This was a very kind old lady, who remains the only person I have ever known who managed to speak by converting every single noun and every adjective into its diminutive, affectionate form. (These grammatical forms only exist in the rich Russian language, as far as I know.) I loved her for it and still do. I still mention her in my prayers!

During the summer-school holidays, Lidia Ivanovna moved with my half-sister and me to the Dashevskaya summer house/*datcha* on the opposite bank of the Sungari River, which was reserved for *datchas.* This was considered to be a top-of-the-list *datcha,* even though it had no electric power supply and no indoor washing and toilet facilities, all of which really did not detract from my joy of living there. In fact, these were the very best times for me. I spent all day in and around the water and eventually taught myself to swim. Year after year, I used to get an extremely dark-brown suntan, which is a bit of a health risk for me now.

Unfortunately, I also did a lot of fishing, which, being a vegetarian now, I seriously regret and am deeply ashamed to admit. Not harming or taking the life of any living creature is a very basic belief of all members of the Toren family, which, no doubt, will be passed on by Laura to her children. This respect for all life extends to all insects, large and small, including large cockroaches—I have been chosen to catch them and release them into the front garden. Even though I have gained considerable skill and experience over the years in catching them, I must admit that very often they manage to outwit me.

We had a ginger cat, whose name I do not remember—possibly Mirka. She used to catch mice that came down to our place from the roof space, especially during the cold season. We also had a very large dog, Batar, the unchallenged strongest dog in Birgevaya Street, who looked like a St Bernard except for his shorter fur. I was told that a drunken Japanese officer killed him with his sword, but I never believed that story. We also had two young dogs, Chiro and Kooro (White and Black in Japanese). They mysteriously disappeared without any explanation. I always suspected my stepfather behind these disappearances. He also got rid of the guinea-pigs that I was raising with an adult friend. What we were left with were our golden canary birds and white rice birds. The canaries laid eggs and raised their chicks.

Sungari is a very wide river that flows into the Russian river, Amur. Sungari has a high, steep bank on the city side, reinforced with large rocks, and a low, sandy bank on the side where the summer houses are located. By the end of each summer, when the water level rose due to the gradual melting of high mountain snows upstream, it flooded the low bank, and the river's width would exceed eight hundred metres. The Sungari water was not clear, probably because of the clay bottom, strong current, and uneven depth.

One day, when I was about thirteen years old, we were sitting on a yacht, anchored close to shore, together with two girls of the Orlov family who lived in the same *datcha* complex as we. As I was talking to the older sister, the younger six-year-old girl suddenly slipped off the edge and was instantly swept under the yacht by the river's current. Luckily, I saw it and was able to dive after her and deliver her safely into the arms of her very grateful mum. A few years later, I managed to rescue a fellow who got into trouble with the river's current, by swimming out to him and talking him safely back to shore.

I enjoyed the very beautiful sunsets upstream over the river but cannot recall in which season they were the most beautiful. I also recall the awesome sight of the thick winter ice melting partially and then breaking up in spring, with huge chunks climbing over each other, driven by the strong river current. In winter, the ice was over a metre thick. Each holiday of Russian *Krestchenye*/Christening on the nineteenth of January, a hole was cut in the river's ice, and a net was lowered into the freezing-cold water. During the religious service that followed, elderly religious people jumped into this freezing-cold water which, apparently, could feel warm by comparison to the ambient air temperature of anything between minus twenty and thirty degrees Celsius, especially in windy conditions, in spite of the faster heat transfer through water than through air. After the religious service, bottles were filled with holy water, which was drunk throughout the next twelve months to cure most sicknesses. I do not doubt that it worked and works for people who believe in it. In Hamlet, Shakespeare says, *"There are things on heaven and earth, Horatio, Man was not meant to know."* I believe this to be true.

In winter, I liked most of all to go with my friend, Isiah, to the steep city-side bank of the frozen Sungari, near the yacht club, climb up the wooden stairs to an elevated platform and to sleigh down an ice slope and around an icy 180-degree curve, back to the bottom of the stairs. We did this again and again until it got dark. Great fun!

We also did a lot of ice-skating in the open skating rink in winter on the Commercheskaya Street. Every so often, we had to retreat into the "warming-up hut" (*teplushka*) with a woodfire stove to thaw out our frozen fingers and especially our frozen, aching toes. We also played a primitive version of hockey without sticks by pushing the puck with our skates.

Back to the inhabitants of Birgevaya Street.

Dr. Stasya Basina was Russian-Jewish, born in Harbin, but studied medicine in Belgium. She assisted Dr. W in his practice and acted as interpreter into and from German for the Chinese and Russian patients. When the Japanese imprisoned Stasya, her place was taken by a Catholic nun, Schwester Ida, with a round face, rosy cheeks, and a frozen smile.

Stasya Basina did not like Marfa and me from the very start because, in spite of Dr. W being Jewish, we were not; therefore, we did not fit into her narrow-minded view of the world. She and I only spoke to each other on rare occasions. She had bad teeth because she was scared of dentists. She was even more scared of drowning, so we were royally entertained when she occasionally summoned the courage to cross the Sungari together with her good-looking kept man, Valdemar, and us in a rowboat, seating six people and the Chinese oarsman. Valdemar, who was a larrikin with a healthy sense of humour, used to rock the boat from side to side halfway across the river and then say to her that, should the boat capsize, she should hold on to the bottom of the river. She was screaming in terror, and we were bursting with laughter!

I liked Valdemar, with his sense of humour and outwardly happy nature. I liked playing checkers with him. I also admired him because he did not let himself be disturbed and intimidated by the critical and petty remarks of Dr. W; for instance, Dr. W criticised him for the lack of good table manners, in the way he held the teapot back-to-front when pouring himself a cup of tea. In 1945, after the war ended, when Stasya got herself a Russian Jewish Red Army captain, Valdemar got married and moved to a small railway township, Chaylar, where he committed suicide a few years later.

I also played checkers with Stasya's mentally sick brother, Lyova. He apparently lost his mind as a young man, during his uni days. I felt sorry for him. Lyova suffered from mood swings and a persecution complex, complaining angrily about people following him. Most of what he was saying did not make any sense or was incoherent when he was talking to himself. He was in his late forties, stocky, bald, with small, round glasses and a serious, worried expression on his face. Outdoors, he wore a very old, grey, unbuttoned overcoat, which struggled to keep up with him as he was striding ahead at great speed, possibly trying to get away from his imaginary persecutors. In retrospect, his overcoat reminds me of the one that Inspector Columbo wore in the TV detective series. Lyova spent his time travelling back and forth on the tram without any specific destinations. To be able to buy his tram tickets, he would ask one of us for, say, one hundred yuan. If you told him that you did not have one hundred yuan, he would then ask you for two hundred yuan. From time to time, he had to be bribed to agree to go to the bathhouse (*banya*) with Valdemar. When his sister, Stasya, was eventually allowed by the Soviet authorities to leave Harbin for Israel, she left the 47 Birgevaya Street property to her old aunty, Basya, in exchange for the aunty agreeing to look after Lyova for the rest of his unnatural life.

I do hope that his poor soul found peace and happiness in his next life!

Harbin – 1938

Harbin – 1947

Harbin – 1949

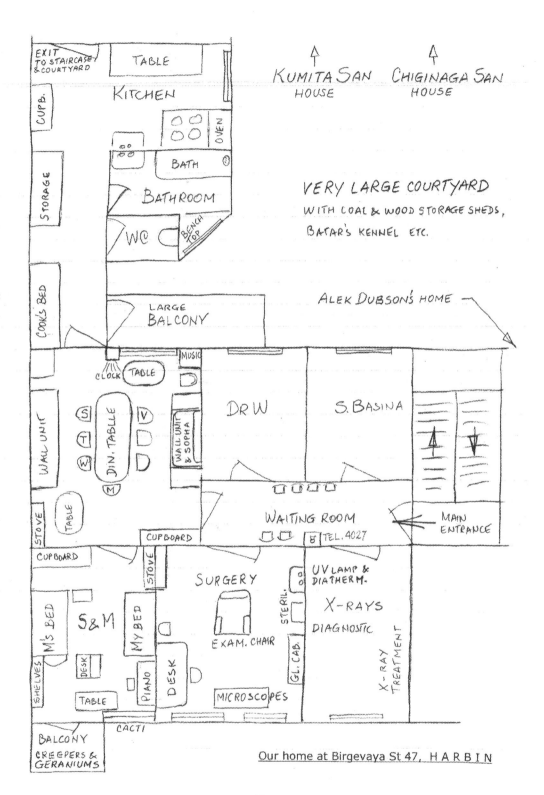

EXIT TO STAIRCASE & COURTYARD

CUPB.

STORAGE

COOK'S BED

TABLE

Kitchen

OVEN

BATH

Bathroom

WC

BENCH TOP

LARGE BALCONY

KUMITA SAN HOUSE

CHIGINAGA SAN HOUSE

VERY LARGE COURTYARD
WITH COAL & WOOD STORAGE SHEDS,
BATAR'S KENNEL ETC.

ALEK DUBSON'S HOME

CLOCK   TABLE   MUSIC

WALL UNIT

S
T
W   DIN. TABLE
M

V

WALL UNIT & SOPHA

DR W

S. BASINA

STOVE   TABLE

CUPBOARD

WAITING ROOM

TEL. 4027

MAIN ENTRANCE

CUPBOARD

STOVE

SURGERY

STERIL.

UV LAMP & DIATHERM.

X-RAYS

DIAGNOSTIC

M's BED   S&M   MY BED

SHELVES

DESK   PIANO   DESK

EXAM. CHAIR

GL. CAB.

X-RAY TREATMENT

TABLE

MICROSCOPES

BALCONY   CACTI
CREEPERS & GERANIUMS

Our home at Birgevaya St 47, H A R B I N

Chapter 6

School—Primary and Secondary

During my first four to five years in Harbin, I attended an English private school that was founded by an Englishman, Mr. Spencer. He disappeared during the first year—probably arrested by the Japanese authorities. After that, all our teachers were Russian, and during recesses, all the children naturally spoke only Russian with each other. The names of our teachers were Mr. Rogov, Mrs. Kistrutskaya, Mr. Boboriko, and Miss Ada. I cannot remember her surname, but I remember that she had beautiful eyes and high cheekbones. The school was not too far from where I lived, so I was able to get there on foot. Eventually, after about four or five years, the Japanese authorities closed the English school down.

Before transferring to the Russian high school, Kolya Peshkovsky (Stasya's nephew) and I had about one year of intensive catch-up private lessons. In those days, Russian primary and secondary education took only a total of ten years, but to make up for this, we attended school six days a week. Now, primary and secondary education in Russia lasts twelve years, the same as in Australia. Kolya and I graduated from high school in 1948 at the age of seventeen. (Kolya studied medicine in Jerusalem, Israel, worked as a medical practitioner in Africa, and died around 1985 from stomach cancer.)

There were four Russian high schools in Harbin, three mixed schools and one exclusively for girls. Soon after the Soviet Red Army occupied Harbin in 1945, all Russian schools came under the direct control of the USSR Department of Education and had to comply fully with its uniform education program and curriculum. This program applied throughout all the fifteen states of the Soviet Union. All examination papers arrived directly from the Department of Education in Moscow. The envelope containing these papers was only opened on the day the examination was to take place, immediately prior to the exam.

I do not remember the address of our school in years seven and eight. During year nine, our Third High School was accommodated in the former commerce school building in the Novy Gorod District, opposite the Railways Club. This was a very large, modern building. In winter, the ink froze solid in the inkwells, so we wore gloves and used pencils. During year ten, our high school moved to Sadovaya Street, also in the Novy Gorod District. All these locations were far away from where I lived. In summer, I rode to school on my Wanderer bike, and in winter I got there by tram and on foot. In spite of the widespread hardships and poverty, people were honest, and I did not have to lock up my bike. I did not even have a chain and padlock. This only just occurred to me whilst writing this account. Before this, I took it for granted. You may not have realised it until now, but we Russkies are good people!

Sitting next to me at school was another Stepan, Stepan Erofeev, with whom I shared my sandwiches that were prepared by our cook, Mr. Wan. Stepan Erofeev did all my technical ink drawings for fifty yuan each. His brother, Sasha Erofeev, dropped out of school after year eight. He was not the studious type and was more interested in constructing small firearms, one of which exploded in his hands and scarred his face but, thank God, spared his eyes.

These were difficult times, and people were struggling to feed and dress their families. Many of my classmates were from poor families. I felt uncomfortable and self-conscious when, having outgrown my trousers or shoes, I had to wear new ones to school. This dislike for new clothes stayed with me for many years.

In front of the two Stepans sat Galina Vorobyeva and the daughter of the Soviet Union's most outstanding general of World War II, Marshal Georgy Zhukov, who successfully defended Moscow and Stalingrad against the Germans and then drove them all the way back to Berlin, where he accepted the German surrender on May 9, 1945. Without the brilliant strategies of Zhukov and the sacrifice of about 12 million Russian soldiers (not counting the wounded), the Germans would not have been defeated and the world, especially Europe, would have been a very different place. Dwight Eisenhower admired Georgy Zhukov as a friend and respected his genius as a strategist. Marshal Zhukov was too successful and became too popular after the war, so Stalin transferred him and his family from Moscow to Harbin.

Allow me, for my own record, to mention some other names of my schoolmates that I can still remember from our last year of study. At the end of our left row of desks were Nikolai Chuan and Tolya Boshko. At the front of the middle row was my favourite freckle-faced Tatiana Skovanova, with high cheekbones and a cheeky smile. At the end of that row were the two lovebirds, Sergey Zanozin and Lena Poliakova. On the other side of the classroom, in the right row, were Mila Keend and some other girls whose names I do not remember at present. Sergey Zanozin's sister, Natasha Zanozina (now Natasha Bucklieva), with whom I worked for many years here in Sydney, was in a class one year below ours.

You can see my classmates and me on the faded photo that Sergey Zanozin was kind enough to send me a few years ago. (Unfortunately, I lost many of my childhood photos when I severed my relationship with Dr. W's family.)

I met up with Natasha Bucklieva again quite unexpectedly at an employees' party soon after I joined BSP Industries in Sydney, just a few weeks after arriving in Sydney in 1963. Twelve years later, she joined my company. Natasha was a brilliant draftsperson and technical illustrator—the very best I have worked with.

Our class teacher was Elena Dmitrievna, who taught us maths. She was nice, but we called her *Zhaba,* which in translation means "toad"—because she looked like one. Believe it or not, I can still clearly hear her squeaky voice and would have no problems recognising it after sixty-six years. Our Russian literature teacher was Vera Stepanovna Apanaskevitch. She also settled in Sydney and continued teaching a weekend Russian school in Strathfield until her late eighties. She passed away a few years ago at the age of one hundred. Our chemistry and Theory of Darwinism teacher was Fedot Semyonovitch Solovyov. If one of the girls failed to answer a chemistry question in class, he used to say that it did not really matter, because this knowledge would not help her anyhow to fry cutlets in her future married life. Apart from this unfortunate sexist remark—typical for those sexist years—he was always very friendly and kind to all of us.

Our gym teacher was Fyodorov, and I did not like him because of his bossy attitude. After our *stodnyovka,* the celebration lunch that traditionally takes place one hundred days before the end of high school, when we all ate Chinese *pelmeni* (meat dumplings) and drank too much vodka, we spotted Fyodorov on the opposite side of the road. Being slightly drunk, I wanted to cross the road and challenge him to a fight, but fortunately, I was prevented from doing so because, as a boxer, he could have beaten me to a pulp with one arm tied behind his back. After the *stodnyovka*, on our long walk home from Novy Gorod to Pristajn, Kolya Peshkovsky and I had to cross the City Park and, as luck would have it, we met and were seen in our drunken state by our Russian literature teacher, Vera Stepanovna. The following day, we had to apologize to her. However, she was very gracious about it all and did not report us to the school principal, Mr. Voyenov.

I was always a diligent, good student, first or second in class, even though I received no support or encouragement whatsoever at home. When I needed help during my high school years, I went to Nikolai Samuilovich Rogov, who was my teacher at the English school. I will always feel a debt of gratitude to him. Unfortunately, at that time I was not mature enough to fully appreciate his generosity. As you will read later on, his support and generosity continued even after my high school studies.

In year nine, I managed to top our class and, together with Mila Keend, was chosen to represent our class at the year ten graduation "White Ball." I was petrified because, being just sixteen, I was afraid of girls and did not know how to dance. So I urgently started taking private dancing lessons from Mr. Belov. He was a very fit, elderly gentleman with white hair and a very large white Cossack moustache. He eventually taught me the waltz, foxtrot, tango, as well as the *kasachok* and Ukrainian *gopak.* I cannot remember exactly what happened, but I know that I did not attend the ball that year after all. I must have given up my position to someone else in my class. The following year, at our own graduation White Ball at the Yacht Club, I took out a girl from the Girls' Second High School, also called Mila, but whose surname I cannot remember.

As mentioned earlier, I graduated from high school at the age of seventeen. Because I did not attend the graduation ceremony, I did not know at that time whether I graduated at the top of my class or in second place. I thought that Sergey Zanozin might have beaten me to first place. I lived in a different part of town from the school and from my classmates, and none of my classmates had telephones. However, a couple of years ago, I found out from Sergey's sister, Natasha, that it was me who topped the class. Both Natasha and Sergey lived in Sydney, and both of them worked as draftspeople in the company I managed in Sydney after we arrived here, but it never occurred to me before to ask them who topped the class.

Both Natasha and Sergey were heavy smokers for most of their lives. Sergey paid the ultimate price for this indulgence. Last year, he had one of his legs amputated, and last month, he passed away. My good friend Natasha suffers from severe emphysema. She is a very brave woman. She lives by herself far away from where I live. Her closest friend in her lonely life is her cat. God bless her and her brother!

Back into the past. During my school days, I took painting lessons from a well-known painter, A.N. Klementyev, who abbreviated his name to Klem whilst working in Paris. A few years later, I attended his funeral, which took place in the large Harbin Cathedral. My next art teacher was Japanese and also studied and worked in Paris.

I took piano lessons from Fira Lev. Every few months, my progress was reviewed by Fira's teacher, Mrs. Gershgorina, who also tested me each time, determining that I had perfect pitch in my hearing. Unfortunately, I did not practice playing the piano enough and stopped my music lessons, having reached my swan song with Ludwig van Beethoven's "Für Elise." If only I knew how much I would regret this in the years to come and for the rest of my life!

Not being able to play the piano now and not speaking Mandarin turned out to be my first two serious regrets in life. Two others followed later.

Although I do not play a musical instrument, music has been the great pleasure of my life. I love all the Russian romantic classical composers—Tchaikovsky, Rachmaninoff, Rimsky-Korsakov, Borodin, Glinka, Glazunov, Mussorgsky; all the Western classical composers—Beethoven, Chopin, Grieg, Schumann, Brahms, Schubert, Mendelssohn, Liszt, Dvorak, Bruch, Paganini. I hope I've not left anyone out! I am sure they would forgive me. Let me quickly add that I also love arias from famous Italian, French, and Russian operas and Viennese operettas.

I had a wonderful experience recently, which I must share with you. I listened to Brahms's Violin Concerto in D Major, Op. 77, performed by a young Japanese virtuoso violinist, Junco Fukada. You may be able to find it on the Internet. The feeling with which she performed this beautiful concerto was absolutely divine. You could hear it, and you could see it in her facial expressions. Her technique for this difficult piece was also amazing. Standing up, she barely reached the height of the seated orchestra violinists around her. The violin looked too large for her delicate body.

Her performance of the second part of this concerto was even more amazing than her performance of the first part. I had tears in my eyes as I was listening with gratitude to this amazing collaboration of Johannes Brahms and Junco Fukada.

Romantic old Russian songs, referred to in Russian as *stariniye romansi* (*старинные романсы*), with their beautiful, sentimental, and melancholy lyrics; Russian wartime songs of the 1940s; some songs from Russian movies; Gypsy songs and old Russian folk songs all have a special place in my heart. When I am alone at home and feeling lonely, I sing these songs to myself. I know the lyrics to many of them by heart.

I also enjoy all the lovely American and English golden oldies sung by Nat King Cole, Billie Holiday, Louis Armstrong, Ray Charles, Dinah Shore, Vera Lynn, Rod Stewart, Elvis Presley, the Ink Spots, the Platters, the Mills Brothers, and Max Bygraves.

I feel sad that the young generation of today is missing out not only on the beautiful melodies of yesteryear's songs but also on the lovely, sentimental lyrics of those songs.

I do not understand and do not enjoy the so-called "modern classical music." I do not even regard it as being music. I feel the same way about so-called modern fine art, which occupies wall space in today's art galleries and insults our intelligence with its pretence.

Not long ago, on our way to uni, our twenty-year-old granddaughter, Laura, told me about some classical-music lectures. I said to Laura that I am only interested in listening to music itself, not to strangers talking about it. After a minute or so, Laura responded, "Dada, you are really a pure music lover." This was a sincere compliment, which I greatly appreciated. In fact, music has become even more important to me since grieving for my wife, Lisa. When I am at home by myself, I listen to music nonstop, all day long. I cannot imagine my life without music.

Year 10 of High School in Harbin - 1948

Chapter 7

Apprenticeship—Uni Will Have to Wait for a Few Years

Having graduated from high school with a very good leaving certificate in 1948, I intended to study mechanical engineering at the Harbin Polytechnic Institute, but my application was refused because, contrary to the vast majority of people, I did not apply for Soviet citizenship. Applying for Soviet citizenship in those days was the norm, but it also meant that you may never be able to leave the Communist bloc of countries or even just travel outside the iron curtain. At that time, in the late 1940s, we could not have imagined in our wildest dreams that this situation would ever change, and that the mighty Union of Soviet Socialist Republics could and would ever disintegrate. In fact, it only happened many years later with Mikhail Gorbachev's *Perestroyka* and *Glasnost* during the late 1980s and Boris Yeltsin's reforms in the 1990s.

When my application to the Harbin Polytechnic Institute was rejected, Mr. Rogov was working at the head office of the Chinese Eastern Railways, which was in control of the Harbin Polytechnic Institute. Once again, Mr. Rogov tried to help me by appealing on my behalf for my application to be reassessed and accepted, but it was again denied. As you can imagine, it took a lot of courage in those days to appeal on behalf of someone who refused to apply for Soviet citizenship! Mr. Rogov was undeniably the best friend anyone could ever wish for.

After the Red Army occupied Harbin in 1945, the Soviet Russian authorities arrested thousands of people amongst those who fled Russia during and after the 1917 Bolshevik Revolution. These people ended up in the Siberian gulags. Kolya's father, Dr. Peshkovsky, was amongst them. He was never seen or heard from again. Apparently, in the various settlements along the railway line, there were hardly any men left. Many of them were Cossacks or descendants of those Cossacks who fought against the Bolshevik revolutionary army in and after 1917.

So, instead of entering uni, I went to work as a milling-machine apprentice at the Bashkirov factory on Vodoprovodnaya Street. After a couple of months, the man responsible for the milling machines got sick with typhus, and I was left to work on my own. Based on what I had managed to learn, I did all right producing different-size gears for automotive gas-generator blowers. In those post-war years, petrol was not available, so cars were fuelled by CO (carbon monoxide) that was generated in these gas generators by blowing air through smouldering wood chips. These gas generators were mounted at the back of motor vehicles with both petrol and diesel engines.

A few months later, I was assigned an apprentice, and I taught him how to cut these gears. The theory of various types of gears fascinated me, so I took private lessons from the Russian factory engineer, who taught me the theory of involute spur, helical, bevel, and worm gears. This turned out to be extremely useful to me in the years to come, especially during my working-student days in Haifa. Twelve years later, in 1960, as a qualified engineer, I learned the design and manufacture of spiral-bevel and hypoid-automotive rear-axle gears in Birmingham, UK.

My weekly wages at the Bashkirov factory of seventy thousand yuan did not amount to very much because of the high inflation. Nevertheless, I gave the money to my stepfather.

Whilst Mr. Rogov was appealing on my behalf, I was still hoping to be accepted to the Harbin Polytechnic Institute. Therefore, I took private lessons in higher maths from the lecturer at the institute, so as not to fall too far behind the students in their first semester. I had to travel to his home in Novy Gorod in the evening; tired after a long day's work, I often dozed off whilst he was lecturing me.

On Sundays, I took driving lessons from a taxi driver. Hardly any people owned cars in those days; therefore, there were no driving schools. Like all motor vehicles, the taxicab was equipped with a large CO gas-generating cylinder, attached to the rear end of the car. When I arrived early in the morning to the private home of the taxi driver, several chores had to be dealt with before we could start the driving lesson. We had to load the gas generator with short pieces of chopped-up wood, light them with burning newspaper, and then blow air through the gas generator by turning the handle of the blower by hand. At the same time, we also had to light a small fire on the ground beneath the engine of the car in order to heat up the oil in the engine sump—otherwise, the engine would not start. It was winter, and the temperature would have been minus 20 degrees Celsius or even considerably less.

Chapter 8

Love at First Sight—It Does Happen!

Strange and unexpected meetings, linking events across continents and generations, do happen in life—and that is not all. Some of these strange and unexpected meetings cannot be fully explained, as you will see towards the end of this unusual but true story.

The city of Harbin grew out of a nineteenth-century Chinese fishing village on the banks of the great Sungari River. In 1897, Russian engineers commenced the building of the Chinese Eastern Railway line and settled in Harbin. During and after the 1917 Bolshevik Revolution, a great many Russians fled their homeland and also settled in Harbin, thereby forming the largest Russian community outside Russia.

We enjoyed a rich cultural life in Harbin, in spite of the prevailing difficult economic conditions during the Second World War. In 1945, the Soviet Russian Red Army "liberated" us from Japanese occupation, and in 1949, Stalin handed Harbin over to Chairman Mao Tse-tung and the People's Republic of China.

In 1947, our Third High School moved into a large building in Novy Gorod that used to be occupied in pre-Soviet times by the commerce school. One day, towards the very end of my penultimate year of high school, I was crossing the large, open square that separated us from the Railway Club, when I noticed a crowd gathering at the entrance to the club. Out of curiosity, I entered the club and its main hall. Only then did I realize that leaving certificates were being presented to the graduates of the Girls' Second High School, located in Modiagow, another district of Harbin. I sat down and started watching a procedure that was awaiting me the following year, when it would be time for me to graduate from my mixed Third High School.

Several teachers were sitting at a long table on the stage, facing the audience. Students were called up by name, one by one. The girls walked up to the stage and along the table, facing the teachers, who shook their hands, congratulating them and handing them their leaving certificates. I was observing it without much interest; I had nothing better to do that afternoon. At the age of sixteen, I was not yet interested in girls—or so I thought.

Another girl walked up to the stage and along the long table, shaking hands with each of the teachers. After receiving her leaving certificate, she turned around towards the audience, smiled, and descended from the stage. Her gentle, pensive smile, her somewhat sad demeanour, and her graceful, smooth walk hit me like a bolt of lightning—this was love at first sight in the true sense of those words! From that day on, I thought of her every day. As I later found out, her full name was Vera Nikolaevna Saurova. I thought of Vera when I woke up every morning and as I was falling asleep at night.

My situation seemed hopeless. Vera was probably eighteen years old, which would make her two years older than me. This was a big deal at that stage of life. How could she possibly be interested in me? Besides, I was very shy, inexperienced, and would not know what to say to Vera or any other girl. The fact that I grew up without a mother probably contributed to my lack of confidence in such a situation.

Vera lived at the end of Kitayskaya Street, not far from the Sungari River Promenade. This was Harbin's main street. Whenever I had time to spare, I would walk up and down the long Kitayskaya Street in the hope of catching a glimpse of her. Vera had beautiful, large brown eyes, a single very long, slightly reddish-brown plait, a mysterious and gentle smile, and a graceful figure and walk. I was told that at school she was nicknamed *Sympatiushka,* which can be translated as "Sympatico."

A year later, I graduated from high school. I also learned how to dance, but I was still shy and, at the age of seventeen, lacked confidence when speaking with girls. On one occasion, I saw Vera and her sister, Nadia, at the Soviet Club on Kommercheskaya Street. Popular music was playing, and young people were dancing. I invited Vera to dance and even exchanged a few sentences with her. I commented on the fact that she came together with her sister, and she responded by saying that I seemed to notice everything.

That was the last time I saw Vera. Soon after that, at the end of 1949, I took advantage of the unique opportunity to leave Communist Harbin for the free world.

During my last day in Harbin, I kept walking up and down Kitayskaya Street, hoping to see Vera for the last time. That was not to be. My love for Vera accompanied me and stayed with me until such time as I met and fell in love with my future wife, Lisa.

———————

Sixty years passed. I was having breakfast, sitting at a small table in a health-food shop and restaurant in Queenstown, New Zealand, waiting for my vegetarian meal to be served. At a table next to mine sat another elderly gentleman, apparently also waiting to be served. When the food arrived, I noticed pieces of chicken in my "vegetarian" meal. As it turned out, my neighbour's order and mine were accidentally mixed up. We exchanged plates and a few friendly sentences. David Nalden told me that he taught the violin and came to Queenstown, where young virtuosi from the New Zealand School of Music would be competing at the QVSS Festival of Chamber Music. I said to him that I had been listening to the Mendelssohn and Tchaikovsky violin concerti on my iPod that very morning. David invited me to attend the annual QVSS Grand Finale Concert that was taking place on January 22. He then asked me about my accent and where I originally came from. I told him I grew up in Harbin, China, that I was Russian, and that my wife was half-Chinese. He replied that he had a very gifted violin student who was also half-Chinese and whose father may also be from Harbin.

Two days later, I attended the last in the series of concerts, the QVSS Grand Finale Concert at the Queenstown Memorial Hall. The seven competing young violinists appeared to be very accomplished musicians. Anna Kiriaev, about eighteen years old, was exceptionally good playing Sarasate's "Zigeunerweisen" with piano accompaniment. This very technically demanding music has to be played with a lot of feeling, gypsy passion, and the typical Hungarian first syllable accent/emphasis. I thought she was brilliant, and I preferred her execution of that difficult piece to that of a professional musician I have amongst my recordings. Anna's Russian surname did not go unnoticed by me. I realised that she must be the gifted violin student that David mentioned to me in the restaurant.

After the concert, David Nalden introduced me to Anna. I congratulated her on her brilliant performance and told her that it would have made Sarasate proud to listen to her. David told her that I was from Harbin, to which she replied that her grandmother was also from Harbin. We exchanged a few more sentences. I thanked her and David, as well as another senior violin teacher from Israel, Yair Kless, for the wonderful experience of this concert and said good-bye to them. David and Yair were close friends since their youth, when they both studied music in Belgium.

It probably did not take me more than ten minutes to get all the way back to my hotel. The weather was miserable, and I ran most of the way, hurrying to get out of the rain. That may have improved the blood circulation to my brain for what followed. When I returned to the hotel, a silly thought started germinating in my mind—what if Anna was the granddaughter of Vera Saurova? This thought did not make much sense and defied logic. Anna's father was Russian; his mother was from Harbin; he grew up and married his Chinese wife in New Zealand. There were thousands of Russian grandmothers from Harbin in the world, so why should Anna's grandmother happen to be Vera Saurova? Being an analytical and logical person, I could not justify why this thought kept annoying me. Nevertheless, as we all know, logical thinking does not always win an argument!

It was late, and I could see through the dark window that it kept on raining. I dressed quickly and went back to the Memorial Hall. On this occasion, I had an umbrella with me. When I got there, both large glass entrance doors were locked; however, in the background, I could see light coming from the concert hall, and I could hear young voices. These were the students celebrating the successful ending of their series of concerts.

I stood in front of the glass door, partially protected by the building and my umbrella, but nevertheless cold and wet, hoping that someone would eventually come out to the foyer and see me standing there. Twenty or more minutes passed. I was beginning to feel silly and embarrassed at the thought of bothering these people—but, on the other hand, the thought of missing this only chance of getting a clear answer and regretting it later was unacceptable to me. So I kept waiting. At last, a lady came out to the foyer, and I knocked on the glass door. When she approached, I told her through the door that I needed to speak to one of the students by the name of Anna Kiriaev. I had a question about her grandmother—it would only take a minute. The lady replied that she would pass my request on to the Artistic Director. After a few minutes, the Director and Anna came out to the foyer and let me in. Speaking with an American or Canadian accent, he introduced himself as Kevin Lefohn. I apologized for troubling them and asked Anna if she knew the maiden name of her grandmother.

"No, I don't," she replied gently.

"And what about her Christian name. Was it Vera?"

"Yes, it was," she replied with interest.

"Did she have a sister called Nadia?"

"Yes, she did."

"And were they half-Chinese?"

"Yes, they were," replied Anna smiling, obviously realizing that her answers identified her grandmother.

These facts confirmed my illogical expectation of finding one out of a thousand Harbin grandmothers. I then turned to Kevin Lefohn and explained that sixty years ago, I was madly in love with Anna's grandmother, Vera Saurova. He looked at me with a surprised expression and asked how it occurred to me that Anna could be the granddaughter of Vera Saurova. I thought for a moment, tried to concentrate, but could not come up with a reasonable answer—and told them that I did not know how it occurred to me.

Then, to change the subject and to praise Anna in the presence of the Director, I repeated my earlier compliment, saying that Sarasate would be very proud indeed of Anna if he could hear her play his "Zigeunerweisen"—and that I hope that he did hear her. Kevin Lefohn turned to Anna and said to her that she could not have asked for higher praise. She smiled with a gentle, humble smile. I thanked them for a beautiful evening and went back to my hotel.

In my hotel room, I rang our daughter and granddaughter at 11:30 p.m. New Zealand time, 9:30 p.m. Sydney time, and briefly told them about my love at first sight sixty years ago and my unusual meeting with my first love's granddaughter today. My daughter asked me the same question Kevin did—what made me think that Anna could be the granddaughter of the girl I was in love with so many years ago? Once again, I could not come up with an answer that would make sense to our daughter and granddaughter.

Two days later, the penny dropped, or so I think. When Anna and I were first introduced after the concert, her voice and her gentle smile and demeanour may have brought back some faint memories of Vera, consciously or subconsciously, even though Vera's and Anna's facial features had nothing in common, as far as I could see. In trying to support this conclusion, I must say that my perception of people and their feelings has always been good—but on the other hand, I hardly knew Vera; I only spoke to her briefly on one occasion during one dance.

I forgot to mention that I also asked Anna where Vera was living now. She said that both Vera and her sister, Nadia, passed away and that at the end of their lives, they lived in Sydney.

It took me all day today to write this account of my unusual experiences in Harbin and Queenstown, sixty years apart. I was aided by my Russian draft that I prepared in New Zealand on the day following Anna's performance. I was also aided by continuous listening for hours to Sarasate's "Zigeunerweisen" on iTunes, by pressing the automatic repeat button.

So now, let me repeat what I said at the very start: strange and unexpected meetings, linking events across continents and generations do happen in life—and *some of these strange and unexpected meetings cannot be fully explained*.

I enjoyed sharing this experience with you, dear reader!

I would have loved telling this story in all its details to my beloved wife, Lisa, who was also half-Chinese. Lisa was my second and, naturally, my most important love—the one and only love of mine for fifty-four years of happy married life and beyond. Telling Lisa about this will have to wait until we meet again on the other side.

Chapter 9

Journey to the "Free World"—
My Second Long Journey

In the 1940's, people behind the iron curtain were still not free to travel. They were not free to leave the Soviet Union, China, or any other Communist countries. People felt trapped, with no hope whatsoever of ever being able to escape to the "free world." Then, at the end of 1949, a *completely* unexpected thing happened. The group of Jews who fled from Germany to Harbin were offered *laissez-passer* travel documents by the newly established Israeli Embassy in Moscow. A *laissez-passer* (from the French for *let pass*) is a one-way travel document issued to stateless people (also referred to as DPs—displaced persons) on humanitarian grounds by a national government or international organization, such as the United Nations. This unexpected blessing happened as a result of one brave, extremely optimistic young musician, Helmut Stern, sending a letter to the newly established Israeli Embassy in Moscow—a letter that nobody in their right mind would have expected to get through the Chinese and Russian censorships, to arrive at its destination in Moscow. There was even less of a chance for a reply then, getting through all that censorship again, back to Harbin—and yet, this is exactly what happened! My stepfather obtained certificates from the chief rabbi of Harbin that his daughter and "son" converted to Judaism and were Jewish (because children whose mother was not Jewish are deemed not to be Jewish from birth). On the strength of these certificates, all three of us obtained the necessary *laissez-passer* transit documents to leave Harbin and travel to Israel. These were free UNRRA tickets for DPs to travel from Communist China to the free world. All this seemed to us and was indeed nothing short of a miracle!

You may well ask at this point, why did Dr. W not convert his daughter and "son" to Judaism many years earlier, bearing in mind that at home we grew up primarily in liberal but nevertheless Jewish surroundings and many of our friends were Jewish? This would have had the advantage for me in particular of having had a bar mitzvah at the age of thirteen and learning to read and write Hebrew at a young age, in preparation for the bar mitzvah. It would have made my life so much easier during my studies for my engineering degree at the Technion in Haifa in the years to come. So why did my stepfather not do it? Strange, to say the least.

Dr. W sold his X-ray equipment to the Chinese authorities; payment was in gold bars. The gold bars were exchanged on the black market for American share certificates. Each of these transactions, I assume, would have involved considerable financial losses. Some of these valuable papers were then rolled up and inserted into a condom, which was then inserted into a shaving-cream tube by opening the folded end of that tube and replacing some of the shaving cream. Some more papers were hidden under the inner soles of my shoes.

On the day of our departure from Harbin late in September 1949, my dear friend and teacher, Nikolai Samuilovich Rogov, appeared at the railway station to say good-bye to me and, in doing so, put himself again in danger by associating with a person leaving the Communist bloc of countries. This may sound somewhat dramatized to a person who grew up in Australia and who takes freedom of speech and association for granted. In those days, there were many informers (*stukachi*), people who spied on their neighbours, friends, and even family members. I did not see anyone other than Nikolai Samuilovich on the platform, because whole families were departing, leaving no one behind to fare them well, whereas family friends were afraid to associate with them publicly.

This was the last time I saw Nikolai Samuilovich. I do not know why and how I deserved such kindness and sacrifice from him. He was a very proper, serious person and a strict teacher. I never heard him joke or saw him laugh. Being a good, diligent student certainly did not qualify me for such ongoing kindness and attention. I can only imagine that he must have sympathized with some of my difficult childhood, whatever he may have known of it. There was a time when he regularly came to our home, trying to teach my stepfather the Russian language. In 1956, after receiving my degree in engineering in Israel, I wrote a long letter to him, and he replied. A few years later, I found out from a common acquaintance that his only son, Kolya, died from TB in Shanghai. Kolya spoke Mandarin fluently and was a very independent individual.

From Harbin, we travelled by train to Tientsin. Some of the countryside was flooded, with both sides of the elevated railway track submerged under water all the way to the horizon. We could see no people or animals, no submerged structures of any kind. It gave one the illusion of ocean travel on a ship, but for the clicking of the train wheels.

Upon arrival in Tientsin, we were accommodated in the "luxurious" hotel, the Savoy, where I promptly found a large scorpion in the washbasin. Soon after our arrival, I contracted hepatitis A, accompanied by severe jaundice. I could hardly eat anything at all until after our departure several weeks later. Throughout my life, I remained very sensitive to rancid oil in food such as nuts.

On the day of our departure from Tientsin to Shanghai on October 27, 1949, all the departing passengers were told to line up with their luggage in a long queue along the wharf's edge. A group of customs officers went from passenger to passenger to inspect them and their luggage. My shoes and the shaving cream did not attract their attention, and we boarded the ship.

We travelled on a former American troop carrier, the SS *Wooster Victory,* under the Panamanian flag, with an all-Italian crew, transporting DPs from Tientsin via Shanghai, Manila, Singapore, Cape Town, Los Palmas, Gibraltar, and Napoli to Haifa. The SS *Wooster Victory* belonged to the Sitmar Line, formed by the Russian émigré, Alexander Vlasov. Sitmar chartered the ship to the IRO, the International Refugee Organization, which was part of the UN.

Not having eaten for several weeks in Tientsin, I was famished and ate all my spaghetti and my seasick friends' spaghetti as we travelled through the stormy waters of the Indian Ocean, around the Cape of Good Hope and through the Gibraltar Straits. Maintaining a full stomach, I never got seasick. I was the only person on deck during major storms. I liked to hold on and lean over the railing at the stern of the ship and watch the two huge propellers lifting out of the "boiling" water and then diving deep down, until the water level was within about three metres or less from the ship's stern deck. It was both awesome and fascinating to watch.

Most of all, I loved to watch the dolphins playing as they raced ahead of the ship's bow, the schools of flying fish, and the beautiful sea turtles. Whilst anchored in Manila

Harbour, in the evening when the water was still, we could see fluorescent silhouettes of what we were told were sharks swimming slowly adjacent to the anchored ship's hull.

On the SS *Wooster Victory,* I met a middle-aged man, a barkeeper from Shanghai who was on his way back to his native Berlin via Haifa. He was a friendly fellow. He was also a chain smoker, and his proud achievement in life was performing the trick of using his tongue to turn the lit end of a cigarette into his mouth, extinguishing it inside his mouth (I don't know how), and then chewing it up and swallowing it—bravo! I told him about my mother who, I assumed, could still be living in Berlin. He promised to try to find her and tell her of my whereabouts.

A few months later, he did manage to locate her through artists' circles, and this is how I established contact with my mother. Ten years later, in 1960, Lisa and I spent time with her and her husband, Erich Otto, in London and Paris, after I completed my six-month engineering assignment in the UK. I never found out if she tried to get in touch with me in Harbin after the end of the war in 1945. Maybe—probably—she did, but her letters could not get through the Soviet and Chinese Communist censorship. She was a proud person who felt no need to justify any of her actions or inactions.

Regardless of what may or may not have happened, I still think of my mother with deep affection. She was an unusual, interesting person, as I found out many years later, when I kept visiting her and her husband in Germany during my frequent business trips to Europe. I look forward to seeing her in my next life and asking her all the many questions that have accumulated in my mind since she passed away, questions that I failed to ask her during those visits. In those years, I was still too preoccupied with my work responsibilities and had not yet reached some of the wisdom and understanding that is only acquired at a much more mature age. Besides, at that stage, I still thought Dr. W was my biological father.

The long voyage from Tientsin to Haifa was a happy time for me, even though, being *laissez-passer* travellers, we were not allowed to disembark in any of the ports where the ship dropped anchor to take on fuel and provisions for our "spaghetti meals." It was a long voyage around Africa, because the captain could not take the shorter route through the Egyptian-controlled Suez Canal with so many Jews on board. It took us precisely two months, departing from China on October 27 and arriving in Haifa on December 27, 1949.

Chapter 10

Israel—A Very Different World

By the time we got through the Port Haifa immigration authorities, it was very late. We were driven in trucks and buses south to the *Shaar Ha'Aliya* (the Gate of Immigration), which was once a British army camp, also known as St. Luke's. We did not get to see anything on the way, because it was pitch dark. December and January are the height of the rainy season in Israel. The weather in the days that followed was miserable, and the clay ground between the barracks was wet, muddy, and slippery. After about a week, we were suddenly transported to another, more permanent camp, about twenty kilometres south of Haifa, adjacent to Atlit with its deserted ancient ruins, which is situated on the shores of the Mediterranean Sea. Atlit's ruins have a rich history going back to the Crusades as one of their last outposts. In the years to come, whenever I was driving from Tel Aviv to Haifa, I used to make a short stopover at these deserted ruins. I do not recall ever seeing any people there, which gave this place an additional special atmosphere.

Back to the Atlit immigrants' camp: same army barracks, same clay ground, and same charm. The highlight of each day were the meals in the *cheder ochel*, the communal eating room, where we were fed more or less the same food every day, sitting around long communal tables, with large black-and-yellow striped wasps descending on several big bowls of bread, olives, jam, and cottage cheese distributed along the tables. We were looked after very well, considering the fact that, at that time, you could not even buy potatoes in Israel.

I made friends with a very nice fellow my age from Harbin, Alec Sandlarovitch. Both he and his sister had bright-red hair and white, sun-freckled skin. Alec was a serious but cheerful person, determined to settle in a kibbutz or *moshav* and to dedicate his life to agriculture. With that in mind and with the prospect of much manual work ahead, he was very concerned about the thin skin on the palms of his hands. A number of times, he examined my strong hands with a deep sigh of friendly envy, pinching the thick, durable skin of my palms.

I do not remember how many weeks we stayed in Atlit. Our next destination was Beith Olim Shimon, an immigrants' camp between Tel Aviv and Holon, next to the Arab village of Abu Kabir, where I occasionally drank Turkish coffee. Beith Olim Shimon was a much nicer camp than the previous two, located on a somewhat hilly terrain. Besides, the miserable, cold, rainy weather had passed, and there was a lively group of young people in the camp from Poland, England, Bulgaria, and China. We met every evening for a friendly chat in the single-room police station in an old, typically Arabic, small whitewashed building close to the entrance to the camp. The only Hebrew-speaking person amongst us was the young, friendly policeman.

Amongst these young people was a young Polish girl, Henya, who used to tell me that if I kissed her eyes, she would never forget me. She had big green eyes. I wonder if she still remembers me. There was also a young, friendly English girl from Manchester, Luella, who liked me. However, I was still thinking of Vera Saurova, and one evening, whilst all the office staff were gone, I drew the unusual profile of Vera on the outside of one of the office doors. It turned out to be a good resemblance. Vera was definitely still there with me!

The camp was surrounded by an old, grey wall constructed out of large, different-size volcanic rocks. Large geckos with dark-grey, spiny skins sat on the wall, sunning themselves, absorbing the sun's energy and nodding their heads. Fortunately for geckos, the weather in summer in Israel is always sunny, with never a single shred of cloud in the sky.

Whilst in Beith Olim Shimon, I did some manual work, such as cutting down tall grass using a hoe, as a deterrent against snakes. I was paid the princely wage of one Israeli lira per day. Accommodation and meals were, naturally, free. Fortunately, I never encountered any snakes. I also occasionally fought grass fires, moved furniture in and out of storage, and so on. Not having heard about the prospect of a bad back, I still felt invincible in those days.

I knew that I would be conscripted into the army for a two-year compulsory service, but that this would only happen one year after my arrival in Israel. This one-year delay was imposed on new arrivals to enable them to learn the Hebrew language or to improve their knowledge of it before joining the armed forces. I had the disadvantage of never having studied Hebrew, compared to all other young men who knew how to read and write, having learned Hebrew before their thirteenth birthday for their bar mitzvahs.

Nevertheless, I decided to do my best to avoid this waste of a whole year, because it was still my firm intention to study mechanical engineering and to start this as soon as possible. To achieve my objective, I travelled to air force headquarters. I managed to find the right person to present my case to, showing him my good high school certificate and telling him about my experience of calculating and cutting gears. He arranged for me to sit for a psycho-technical test, in which I did very well. As a result, I was offered to join the armed forces immediately, with the option of joining the pilot-training course, provided I committed myself to stay in the air force for an additional three years, on top of the two compulsory years. Needless to say, this option did not fit into my plans of studying engineering.

Most importantly, I achieved my objective—against all odds, I was able to enlist without any loss of valuable time!

Chapter 11

Boot Camp, Artillery, Air Force—
Not My Cup of Tea

Very early in the morning, on the fourth of June 1950, I reported to the nominated location in Tel Aviv from where our group of new recruits was driven in military trucks to boot camp. The boot camp for girls was further south. After arriving at boot camp, we were issued serial numbers, uniforms, boots, blankets, etc. and accommodated in tents, where we were "welcomed" by our sergeant, an important fellow with a big opinion of himself.

It did not take me long to realize that the army and I were definitely not compatible. Following orders of narrow-minded corporals and sergeants, just because they outrank you; being deprived of any freedom to make your own decisions, to go where you wanted to go, and to do what you wanted to do was definitely not for me! I also found it most repulsive to observe the majority of fellows in my outfit being natural and consistent crawlers to the sergeant. So, at the end of our one-month training, I refused to contribute any money for a present for the sergeant. This must have been reported to him by one of his happy followers, and he retaliated by not informing me of the arrival of the air force officer to the camp, whose job it was to collect all the recruits to the air force. Consequently, I was shipped off far south to the worst artillery D-camp, and then to H-camp. (It seems to me that I am not allowed to identify any camp names and locations even though all this happened sixty-four years ago.)

The very first thing that happened in D-camp was that the group of new recruits was taken on a long march that lasted several days, laden with heavy backpacks and weapons. We walked all day long; not being used to it, we were completely exhausted at the end of each day. However, the worst part of each day was getting up in the dark, before sunrise, feeling completely drained. Being the middle of summer in Israel, when there is never a single cloud in the sky for several months, it was extremely hot, making it even more difficult to carry the load we were burdened with. On the third or fourth day, people started dropping like flies and being picked up by a truck that was following us.

Strange as it may sound, all this was rather fortunate for me, because I decided there and then that I had to get out of this unit. I was limping on my right foot, and I realized that my flat feet would become my ticket out of this outfit and into the air force workshops that I had targeted from the start. When the time finally came for the truck to actively collect not just the people who were dropping out but also the people who appeared to be struggling, a friendly officer noticed my limp and offered me the chance to get on the truck. I thanked him but refused the offer, saying that I could complete the march back to our camp. I knew this would open the door for me to that officer—and it did.

Upon our return to camp, I asked him for a medical examination of my flat feet and the reappraisal of my physical-fitness classification. Some forms had to be filled out, and within a month or two, I appeared before a panel of three doctors, who confirmed my flat feet and reclassified me from first-class to third-class fitness. As a result of this, I was reassigned to the supplies store. That was step one completed!

Now I had to get to the air force headquarters somehow. My first chance presented itself a couple of months later when, working in the supplies store in H-camp, I managed to accompany a truck driver who was making a delivery to a camp in that area. After arriving there, I talked the driver into driving past the air force headquarters building and wait for me whilst I did what I had to do. Without an official army pass, I managed to get past the guard and into the building. Having found a relevant office, I related to the person in charge that I was accidentally overlooked in boot camp and transferred to the artillery division in the far south.

All this had to be accomplished in my very basic Hebrew, supplemented with some Russian, English, and German. A few weeks later, I had to repeat this manoeuvre once again, but on that occasion, although I still had no official army pass, I already knew what to do and how to do it.

Some weeks later, my transfer documents arrived in the H-camp. The friendly officer I mentioned earlier was obviously impressed by this unusual air force request for my transfer and asked me if instead I would consider joining the officers' course. Well, that was an easy choice for me *not* to make. Shortly after that, I arrived in the air force camp, still wearing my artillery green uniform and black cap.

Mission accomplished, in spite of all the difficulties and my considerable language barrier.

For the rest of my military service, whenever I told people that I was able to transfer from artillery into the air force, they found it hard to believe. Thinking back, I too find it hard to believe—but then, I guess, all it took was strong determination and a bit of luck.

The day after my arrival at the air force technical base, I was already in the mechanical workshop at an old milling machine. The beautiful new milling machine, the Jaspar Belgique, was operated by a civilian worker. Nevertheless, I was deliriously happy to be there and to be working on my old milling machine. Without exaggeration, it was a dream come true for me. A couple of months later, the civilian worker left, and I inherited the new Jaspar Belgique milling machine. Who could ask for more?

For the next eighteen months, I worked very closely with Chaim Petraro, an excellent tradesman from Romania; Rafaelo Rachamim, a brilliant turner from Bulgaria; Chaim Ackerman, a Sabra (born in Israel); and Menachem Gotlieb from Hungary. The five of us became very close friends, like the five musketeers. Chaim Petraro was the oldest and most mature and experienced amongst us. Rafaelo Rachamim, who was nicknamed Lulu, was an exceptionally kind, mature, and positive-thinking person. He stuttered heavily, and during his strong stuttering spells could not control his walking steps. In spite of that, he actually volunteered to join the armed forces.

The two sergeant majors in charge of our mechanical workshop, Avraham from Austria and Yehuda from Hungary, were very nice people, and we got along very well with both of them. Captain Levy, in charge of all the different workshops, was not as nice. In spite of this, I managed to avoid all the ridiculous, degrading marching and drill, by insisting that my health records identified my flat feet and that this prevented me from participating in those drills. Captain Levy could see through this ploy and challenged me on the grounds that I proved capable of standing all day at the milling machine. I stood my ground by saying that it may indeed be better for my feet if I stopped working at the milling machine as well. My bluff was effective—I kept on working but did not attend a single one of those dehumanising drills.

We had a cinema in our air force camp, to which most people gravitated in the evening. This is where I saw my first American movies (in Harbin, all movies were, naturally, Russian). Girls from the women's boot camp, which was adjacent to our camp, also came to the movies on weekends—and that is where I first spoke to my future wife, Lisa Dju. I saw her sitting all alone and approached her, introduced myself, and said that I saw her walking in Nathanya, where she lived before being conscripted. Lisa asked me for something to read, and I lent her the book *1984* by George Orwell. This happened in 1952, two weeks before my discharge, sixty-two years ago. The year 1984, depicted by Orwell in his book, seemed very far in the distant future—and yet, 1984 came and went long ago, and here we are in 2014, with Lisa and I getting married in 1955, having been married for fifty-four years, and with Lisa passing away four years and seven months ago, in 2009, at the age of seventy-six. Time flies!

(Laura, when your children read this, they will naturally feel that all these events of 1952, 1955, 1984 and 2009 had all taken place a very, very long time ago! Mind you, this is not how Lisa and I felt about it until recently, when Lisa and I were still together. Now that Lisa is gone, I too feel that all this was very long ago, because I have nobody to share all our memories with. This is also part of the reason why I feel compelled to write about it.)

I was discharged on May 20, 1952, which happened to be my stepfather's birthday. I forgot to mention that my serial number was 169674, and that I reached the high rank of corporal in the mechanical workshop. Two most interesting coincidences happened, in that one of my Harbin friends, Isya, who was recruited many months after me, was discharged the same day as I, and that his serial number happened to be 199674, making him exactly the thirty thousandth recruit after me. He was discharged prior to the expiration of the normal two-year compulsory service because, being unable to cope with army discipline, he deserted and came to me for help. After referring to my stepfather's medical books, I was able to help him act the part of a mentally disturbed person (which he may have been to some degree), in order to avoid military prison as a deserter. Isya died in Sydney in 1976 at the age of forty-four after a heart attack.

My plan of joining the armed forces as soon as possible after arriving in Israel saved me valuable time before enrolling at the Technion, the Israel Institute of Technology, in Haifa. Spending my compulsory military service time in the mechanical workshop gave me practical experience that was of immeasurable value to me, not only at uni, but also throughout my professional career as a mechanical engineer. It also enabled me to earn money during my student years to get me through uni, by working in metal workshops during summer breaks. Unfortunately, I did not use my free time in the air force in the evenings to study Hebrew writing and reading, which could have made my studies in Haifa so much easier. That was not like me at all—I was acting out of character. No excuses!

Chaim Ackerman and Menachem Gotlieb remained close friends after their discharge and opened a workshop in partnership in Ramat Gan. After we got married, Lisa and I became good friends with Chaim Petraro and his wife, Silvia. Lulu visited us a few years later to introduce his young bride. He joined his father and brothers in their workshop in Tel Aviv.

As you can see, Laura, Harbin, and Israel were very different from each other, and life in both Harbin and Israel was completely different from our present life in Sydney. Apart from being very different places, it was also a different time and a very different world—but wait, there is more to come!

Chapter 12

Uni—Once Again—Life Was Not Meant to Be Easy!

When I was rereading and editing this chapter, I found much of it quite funny. I hope that you will enjoy the humour in many of the experiences described here.

After my discharge from the air force on May 20, 1952, I travelled to Haifa and applied for entry into the mechanical engineering faculty of the Technion. Thanks to my good Russian high school certificate, I did not have to pass any entry exams. My next task was to find a job until the start of the first semester and to save enough money for the first year of study.

I found a job at a general engineering workshop in Tel Aviv where, amongst other things, they specialized in the production of spur and helical gears, ranging from very small ones, about twenty millimetres in diameter, to very large cast-iron gears for pumping stations, up to about one metre in diameter. All these gears were custom-made replacements of worn or broken gears, i.e., orders for one gear at a time, so that each old sample gear that came in had to be carefully inspected, measured, and calculated. When I applied for the job, the owner who interviewed me was surprised at my knowledge of gears and gear calculations, because this is a specialized field, with few people (even amongst engineers) having any practical experience in it. As you may recall from a previous chapter, I took private lessons from a Russian engineer at the Bashkirov factory in Harbin.

This workshop had two gear-hobbing machines, one a very small machine and the other a very large one. Both were located in a separate enclosed area below street level. The large machine was extremely noisy, and I was exposed to it for about ten to twelve hours a day. Years later, I realized that the hearing in my left ear, which faced that machine, was affected by the noise; I lost most of the ability to hear higher-frequency sounds with that ear. I was not aware of it bcause the good right ear was compensating for the left one.

During the few months that I worked there, I stayed at Marfa and her husband's place in the small town of Ramat-Gan, close to Tel Aviv. They were renting a room, sharing the kitchen and bathroom with the old, widowed landlady. Marfa worked as an assistant pharmacist, and her husband, Enko, as a draftsman at Mekorot, Israel's water-management company. All three of us slept in the same room.

Finally, the day came when I moved to Haifa. The first year of study was hard, especially because of my poor knowledge of the Hebrew language, *Ivrit,* as it was known. Fortunately, in the first year, I was able to submit my work in Russian for some of the subjects, where the lecturers were originally from Russia.

My living quarters were substandard and certainly not suitable for studying. I shared half a barrack with two truck drivers in an abandoned British army camp that was converted into a *beith chalutzim*, a hostel for young men. The space between the barracks was overgrown with tall grass—a haven for mosquitoes. They invaded our quarters after sunset. In the evening, the walls were covered with mosies, waiting for us to lie down and for them to be fed; we did not have to aim when hitting the walls with our pillows. In addition, the metal legs of our beds were standing in water-filled tins to prevent bedbugs from crawling up into our beds—or so we thought. In reality, I think, it would have stopped them from leaving our beds, assuming they had any intention of leaving what was to them a perfectly good feeding ground. The metal beds and the water-filled tins were the only furniture in our barracks. There was no table and no chairs.

The camp was adjacent to the cement factory of Nesher, half an hour's bus ride north of Haifa. In the open, grassy area not far from our barracks was a tap from which we took water, which was brownish in colour and muddy in taste.

The two truck drivers in my half of the barracks and the people behind the partition in the other half did not occupy their minds by reading books in silence. Instead, they spent their time in loud, idle conversation and laughter, all of which was not conducive to my concentration whilst trying to study!

Every week, I went to the management office of this *beith chalutzim* and paid 4.00 Israeli liras for the privilege of staying there. This was dirt-cheap rent for dirt-cheap accommodations. I knew that I could not possibly stay there for the second year—and I did not.

During our three-to-four-month-long summer breaks, I worked twelve-hour shifts as a toolmaker and gear-cutter. This further enhanced my practical experience in engineering. In the fourth year of my studies, I qualified for a very small scholarship (with the emphasis on *very*), donated by a South African family. I also took small loans from time to time from loan sharks at very high interest (once again, with the emphasis on *very*), which I repaid during the following working summer break or after finishing my studies.

The dean of the Technion was, I believe, a retired military man. He instituted an iron discipline at the Technion, whereby we had four major subjects and several secondary subjects each year, i.e., within two semesters. If you failed just a single major subject during the annual exams, you had to repeat *all* major and *all* secondary subject exams in spring. If you failed any of the major subjects in spring, even a subject that you passed the first time, you had to repeat the year. If you do not understand the logic of this system, don't worry—nobody else did. This was terrifying for students like me who had to work during the summer break, rather than study and repeat all the exams.

Examination papers, with many questions and problems to solve, were always difficult to complete within the allocated time. I was disadvantaged because my reading and writing of Hebrew were very slow. The Hebrew alphabet does not include vowels. Vowels can be identified by dots and strokes, but this tedious practice is reserved for young children's books. The vowels *o* and *u* use the same symbol, unless you choose to add a dot on the side or on top, which nobody does. Besides, there are two different Ts that sound exactly the same and two different Chs that sound similar to choose from. I must have been the only illiterate person who managed to obtain an engineering degree with honours from the Technion. To compensate for my illiteracy, I excelled in my projects of machine design and in subjects that did not require much reading and writing Hebrew, where I could refer to Russian, English, and German books. Fortunately, I never failed a major subject. I did fail one secondary subject, namely steam engines, because I did not have time to attend the lectures, but I passed it the second time. Is it any surprise that I am still having nightmares about failing exams, but less and less frequently as the years roll by? (Nevertheless, believe it or not, I would gladly have more nightmares again, if it was possible to wind the clock back by, say, ten, twenty, thirty, or forty years!)

Before commencing the second year of my studies, I was able to find excellent accommodation on the slopes of Mount Carmel, on the fifth floor (no lift), less than ten minutes' walk from the Technion, with a view of the golden dome of the nearby Baha'i Temple and the Haifa harbour in the distance. I shared the room with Moshe, who came to Israel as a child from Syria. Our landlord's son, Avraham, Moshe, and I were in the same year of the mechanical engineering faculty. We became good friends and were able to support each other in our studies with our different strengths and talents.

Avraham graduated from an excellent French school in Beirut, Lebanon, with exceptional emphasis on maths. He excelled in higher maths, thermodynamics, and similar theoretical subjects. His Hebrew was very good too. When I got stuck with a problem in maths or thermodynamics that I could not solve, I went for help to Avraham. He used to thoughtfully take a piece of paper and a pencil, read the question, concentrate intently for a minute or two whilst making low snort-like noises through his nose—and then, with perfect logical deductions and beautiful pearl-like handwriting, write down line after line of equations, ending up with the solution. Once a problem was solved by him, it looked simple and indisputable. When, on occasion, I would say to him, "Avraham, *sometimes* you are a genius," he would reply in a serious tone of voice that he would prefer me to say that only *sometimes* he was *not* a genius.

My main strength was in subjects, such as descriptive geometry, which requires visualisation at which I excelled, and in machine design and engineering drawing, which was greatly assisted by my practical workshop experience and knowledge of metal-machining practices.

Moshe's main attribute was sheer persistence. I can still see him in winter with his deep, knitted woollen cap pulled all the way down to his eyebrows and over his ears, so that only his bulging inflamed eyes; thin, long nose; and thin, pale lips in his thin, very pale face were visible, trying hard to understand what he was reading over and over again. Having graduated from an Israeli high school, Moshe's Hebrew was perfect (as far as I could judge). He loved to make fun of my poor Hebrew, which I did not really mind. Moshe was an army officer whose education at the Technion was paid for by the army.

The landlord's family was a strange mixture of personalities. The mother was a middle-aged, overweight, intelligent, and kind woman who used to look after me when I got sick with colds and flu. The father was an old taxi driver, who could be heard through two closed doors, swearing in long, repetitive Arabic expletives until he ran out of breath. This used to embarrass poor Avraham, who obviously took after his mum and was a very well-brought-up young man with refined tastes. Avraham did not use sheets as part of his bedding—he said that they felt too cold. In addition, he did not like to stay too long in the bathroom, because he said that he got lonely there.

Avraham corresponded with two French girls—one in Paris, called Monique, and the other, whose name I don't remember, somewhere else in France. He wrote meticulous love letters to them in his exquisite handwriting. One day, having written to both of them, he mixed up the envelopes, thus losing both his girlfriends in one go! That was very sad.

Avraham had three sisters. The oldest sister was married to a naval officer, and they frequently visited her parents. The whole family used to gather in the large living room, engaging in loud conversations, which only occasionally were interrupted by the father's outbursts.

The second sister, a teenager called Alisa, a very nice girl, spoke and argued most of the time in French with her brother, so I could only sense the emotions but not the substance of these arguments. Alisa also married a naval officer—introduced, I assume, by her brother-in-law.

The third sister was a little girl called Yvonne, for whom I drew pictures of animals. Sometimes we got into an argument, for example, when I told her that our beds were infested by bedbugs, which she denied. So we ended up making a bet, which I easily won by exposing any one of the seams of my mattress, where the evidence was hiding.

I must not forget to mention another well-represented insect species. When I entered the kitchen at night, I could not see the cockroaches in the dark, but there were so many of them that I could sometimes hear them rustling before I turned on the light! I am not absolutely sure if I did actually hear them or if I just imagined it.

Occasionally, one of the other students visited us. Frenkel was a student, born in Hungary, who usually spoke with a cigarette holder in his mouth, with or without a cigarette in it. Upon Frenkel's departure, the three of us—Avraham, Moshe, and I—used to rush out to the balcony, equipped with a variety of vessels filled with water, which we dumped on Frenkel as he was hurrying down the last flight of external steps. Since the water was coming down from the fifth floor, it dispersed into many drops over a wide range, which usually hit the target, accompanied by our roaring laughter. This was a healthy distraction from our studies.

For lunch, Moshe and I used to go to a private home that catered for students and others with limited financial means. The family consisted of an elderly, music-loving German-Jewish couple and their daughter, in her early sixties. The conversation around the table was usually about classical music. I do love classical music, but I never took part in these discussions, because Moshe and I were busy filling ourselves with bread, which was deliberately served old and dry to reduce its consumption.

I stayed with Avraham's family until the completion of my studies in Haifa at the end of 1956. The post-graduate studies I did the following year in Tel Aviv.

Avraham visited Lisa and me when we lived in Nathanya. The last we heard of Avraham was that he took up the position of lecturer at the University of Brussels in Belgium.

The last time Lisa and I saw Moshe was when he visited us in Tel Aviv in 1960. He came to ask for my advice whether to accept an offer from the secret service, Mossad, for a dangerous assignment in Syria. Having been born there, he was still fluent in Arabic. It was a difficult decision for him, because he found it hard to refuse a challenge. I don't know what he finally did decide, but I hope that he had the courage to refuse that challenge.

Chapter 13

Wedding Bells—Happy Days!

In one of the earlier chapters, I described to you how Lisa and I first met in 1952 at the air force cinema and how I gave her Orwell's futuristic book, *1984.* When Lisa and I were reminiscing about it half a century later, neither Lisa nor I knew if we still had that book.

About six months after my discharge, we met by chance on the beach of Nathanya. Lisa told me that she was hungry, and since neither of us had any money with us, I managed to get a sandwich from the beach kiosk on credit, with the promise of later payment. I had perfected this approach in Haifa at times when I ran out of money. I always honoured my commitments and thereby earned a good credit rating for future occasions.

A short time later, we met again at the wedding of Lisa's friend, Rosa Leibowich, whom I was dating prior to that and who dumped me because, being a student, I was not a good prospect for marriage.

I started coming to Nathanya on Friday evenings to visit Lisa and take her out to the cinema. After the cinema, Lisa and I used to go to a park called Gan Hamelech (The King's Garden), situated adjacent to Nathanya's beach. The park was about six metres above sea level, and there must have been a spectacular view of the moonlit Mediterranean Sea—but who cared for views when the park had many benches to be occupied by lovers. Our favourite bench was at the very end of the park—possibly reserved for us.

Lisa lived with her mother in Gan Bracha (which translates to *Garden of Blessing—* a complete misnomer!). This "Garden of Blessing" outside Nathanya provided new immigrants with very basic rental accommodation in small wooden semis, consisting of two adjacent units, one room and a kitchen each, with a shared shower and toilet between these two units. At that time, Lisa was still in the army, working in the supplies stores. Her camp was situated not far from Nathanya and Lisa had a pass to come home every day to this Garden of Blessing. Lisa's mother earned a living by crocheting doilies and gloves. She also sold her little oil paintings. Lisa helped her mother with crocheting in the evening and on Saturdays.

This may be an appropriate time to confide something that I did not have the heart to tell Lisa. Many people in Israel suffered financial hardship. Lisa and her mother were no exception; and yet, after every weekend, before I returned to Haifa, Lisa gave me a small Austrian *Kugelhupf* cake to take along, which she had baked lovingly for me. This was very generous, bearing in mind that the ingredients of eggs, butter, sugar, cocoa, flour, etc. were scarce and expensive. This went on for weeks and months, and eventually the time came when I started giving most of these weekly cakes to Moshe because I could no longer eat them. The dilemma: would it have been kinder to tell Lisa to save her the unnecessary expense, or not to tell her, so as not to hurt her feelings? I still don't know.

The following year, we had a formal ball at the Technion to which I naturally invited Lisa. Her mother sewed Lisa a light-blue formal, ankle-long ball gown with a tulle overskirt. Lisa was beautiful. We were very much in love! We danced; we rode a giant wheel, and it started to rain whilst we were on our way to the top. We went to a coffee shop—and around midnight returned to Gan Bracha by sharing a taxi (with two rows of back seats). Sharing the taxi with strangers did not stop us from smooching in the rearmost seats.

My stepfather paid eight hundred Israeli lira "key money," as was customary in those days, to rent a two-room flat with two small, enclosed balconies at 43 Disengoff St. in Nathanya and start practicing medicine again. When I came to Nathanya on weekends, I slept on the couch in the surgery and studied in one of these small, enclosed balconies.

As already mentioned briefly, Marfa, Stasya, and Dr. W combined forces in trying to split Lisa and me up. The first attempt was made by Marfa inviting two complete strangers, a young, eligible Tel Aviv girl and her father, to visit Dr. W in Nathanya on a Saturday. As usual, I was expected to visit Lisa and my stepfather in Nathanya that weekend. Lisa and her mother were also invited to visit Dr. W, because that was naturally what I always expected to happen, since seeing Lisa was the main reason for my weekend visits to Nathanya. Marfa and her collaborators were hoping that I would be attracted to that Tel Aviv girl. As fate would have it, I had to complete an urgent project that Saturday, and therefore I had to stay in Haifa. Since we had no phones, either in Haifa or in Nathanya, I could not inform them of my change of plans—and so their first planned intrigue failed. It would have failed anyhow, even if I had visited them that day. Lisa told me that as the girl and her father were leaving, Stasya said to the girl that she should come again and go to the beach with me. She then turned to Lisa and added, "Naturally, you could come along too if you wish."

Getting rid of Lisa was particularly important to Marfa at that point in time. She and her husband were planning to move to Germany, and she wanted me to come to Germany as well. This did not mean she wanted me to marry the other girl or any other girl. She was only using this other girl to achieve her *current* objective to get rid of Lisa. Had I gotten close to the other girl, she would then have to get rid of that girl as well. She could only deal with one girl at a time. Marfa's and my German restitution money would have combined nicely during the settling-in period in Berlin. Well, it did not work—tough luck!

In July 1955, before the end of my last year of study, Lisa gave me an ultimatum to get married—and so we did. Certain formalities had to be completed and paid for at the town hall in Haifa. We were given the date of August 14. In those days, all marriages in Israel had to be performed at a *Rabbanut;* there were no civil marriages—strange but true. To pay for some of the expenses, I sold a gold signet ring that I brought with me from China.

And so, on the morning of August 14, the wedding party took off by train from Nathanya, bound for Haifa. The party consisted of three people: the bride, the bridegroom, and the bride's mother. After arriving in Haifa, we picked up the documentation from town hall and then took a taxi to the *Rabbanut,* which happened to be right next to the

Technion. Before going to the *Rabbanut,* I quickly ran down to a shop on Herzl Street to rent a *kipa*, or skull cap, for one hour. Rental charge: one lira. We then presented ourselves at the *Rabbanut* where, after some short formalities, the wedding ceremony was conducted on the flat roof of that building under a *chupa,* in the presence of some witnesses who were seconded from the *Rabbanut*'s admin office. Since details of our parents had to be recorded, we invented a Jewish name for my mother, Shoshana.

After the ceremony, the three of us celebrated by having lunch at the Bistro restaurant on Herzl Street. Ever since then, Lisa and I have been of the firm opinion that weddings can be kept simple and that the money saved can be spent wiser by the newlyweds. However, this did not really apply to us in any case because, although we did not spend any money on our wedding, neither could we save any money, because we did not have any money to save! What matters is having a happy married life following the wedding—and we proved it to ourselves in our fifty-four years of happy married life together!

I still had to finish my last semester. Therefore, after the wedding, I stayed in Haifa, in the room that I shared with Moshe, whilst Lisa kept living with her mother in Gan Bracha. I visited Lisa on Saturdays, and we stayed together in a small hotel. The year was 1955. Lisa was twenty-two, and I was twenty-four years old. We were both virgins when we got married. Times were different from now, and so were we.

Our wedding 1955

My beautiful wife, Lisa

Nathanya beach

Chapter 14

The Betrayal—So Be It!

Even after we informed my family about our marriage that had taken place in Haifa, it did not discourage their desperate efforts to have Lisa and me separated. Neither my stepfather nor Marfa had the courage to face me and speak to me about their concerns. My stepfather was in poor health and probably could not be bothered to do so, whilst Marfa had no legitimate arguments to present to me in support of her objection to Lisa and our marriage, knowing consciously and subconsciously that her objection was based solely on her selfish financial aims. The only 'honest' person in their camp was Stasya, who asked me before we got married why I would want to marry a Chinese woman; why didn't I just live with her? I think that was the last time Stasya and I spoke to one another.

When I was visiting my stepfather, he used to let me read letters from Marfa, who by then was already in Germany with her husband, Enko. The first letter he showed me had a page missing. Strange as it may seem, the second letter also had a page missing. When I eventually became suspicious of what was going on, I searched for and discovered the missing pages of his secret correspondence with Marfa in his desk, which provided me with written proof of their conspiracy. I immediately broke off my relationship with both of them. My relationship with Stasya had already been severed prior to that. As a result, I was not even informed of my stepfather's death and funeral six years later.

Since Marfa and I grew up without a mother and with a father/stepfather who was unable to compensate for her absence because of his coldness, it was only natural for Marfa and me to become very close as we were growing up. We shared one bedroom, one wardrobe, one collection of musical records and never quarrelled about anything.

As already mentioned, she and I were very different, not only in appearance but also in character. In retrospect, I must say that she was a rather shallow, superficial person; she did not excel in her studies, in her music, or in her drawing and painting. She went through a large number of boyfriends and confided in me about all the highs and lows of her romances. I was a good, commiserating listener, and occasionally whistled the area of Valentine in Faust, in sympathy with his sister, Marguerite.

Above all, I was a very loyal and dedicated brother throughout our childhood, adolescence, and adulthood. She probably wanted to keep on taking advantage of me, especially when it came to my earning prospects—which were better than her husband's—as well as my German restitution money, the receipt of which was imminent. Therefore, my marriage to Lisa really did not fit into her future plans. As the secret correspondence revealed, her intention was to somehow lure me to join her in Germany away from Lisa, initially at least for a short time, knowing that Lisa would not be able to join me and abandon her mother in Israel.

Whereas I supported Marfa all the way, as always, when she got secretly married without telling her father, she repaid me by organising the visit of a girl and her father from Tel Aviv, people we'd never met before, trying to undermine my relationship with Lisa before we got married. With this first intrigue having failed, she then joined forces with Stasya (who always felt hostile towards Marfa and me) in trying to separate Lisa and me *after* we got married.

In spite of my close relationship with Marfa and my natural expectation of her reciprocal loyalty, her betrayal did not cause me any deep disappointment. Having seen the written evidence, I accepted it as a matter of fact. There was nothing I could do or wanted to do about it. I immediately broke off my relationship with Marfa and Dr. W and never looked back. The loyalty that I felt for them until then evaporated when I realised the injustice and pain they intended to inflict on Lisa, after having witnessed the kind and gentle person she was during the two years of regular weekend visits, as well as their disrespect and disregard for my feelings. The fact is that by totally accepting the situation straight away, it did not cause me any pain.

Whilst spending time with our mother in Berlin, Marfa started an intrigue between our mother and her loyal, older husband, Erich, with the objective of breaking up their marriage. Her tactic must have been to divide and conquer. She was exposed and promptly rejected by our mother. Once again, her objective was financial gain. Erich took her to court to punish her where it must have hurt most—demanding the return of all the money and expenses for Marfa and her husband since they arrived in Germany.

When Marfa and I were small children and we still lived all together in Berlin, one of my mother's sisters, Marie, who lived all her life in Poland, visited us. Our aunt called me *Małpeczka* ("little monkey" in Polish). After spending some time with Marfa and me, our aunt said to our mother that her son was a good boy but that the daughter was no good. At that time, my mother rejected her sister's harsh judgment and was angry with her. Many years later, my mother had to admit that her daughter did grow up to be an evil, selfish individual.

Almost fifty years later, Marfa found out our Sydney address and got her daughter to write to me, in an obvious attempt to restore the relationship. I just ignored the letter; this chapter was definitely and irrevocably closed many years before.

Dr. W apparently died from a second stroke whilst Lisa and I were still in Israel, but I was only informed about his demise much later by my dentist in Sydney. This dentist also left Harbin for Israel and then settled in Sydney.

It is a safe assumption that I was not informed of my stepfather's death because Marfa and Stasya preferred not to share the rather substantial inheritance with me. Dr. W received a large restitution payment from the German government a few years earlier, to compensate him for his loss of medical practice and property in Berlin as a result of Nazi persecution.

A few years later, we heard from a mutual friend in London, Alec Faiman, that Marfa's husband, Enko, died from a heart attack in his early or mid-forties and that Stasya collapsed and died at the bus station in Nathanya. I do not know if Marfa is still alive.

About a year ago, I told Iris that I had forgiven my stepfather, except for the injustice against Lisa in which he was complicit. I would be disloyal to Lisa if I forgave him for this, unless such forgiveness came from both Lisa and me together. Since Lisa is no longer here with me, I cannot put this question to her. Lisa and I were shown a letter that he wrote to the parents of Marfa's husband, in which he expounded on his racist views, stating that the Chinese are inferior to the Japanese, in reference to Lisa being half-Chinese. Nevertheless, I feel sorry for him, for the type of person he was and for his final sickness, misery, and blindness at the end of life, as I was told. That said, I would not like to meet him in my afterlife, because of some vague feeling of disgust towards him since my childhood.

In an earlier chapter, I mentioned that my stepfather "mellowed with age and poor health in his seventies in Israel, and that I was kind and considerate to him until the time that I severed my relationship with him, Marfa, and Stasya." Let me give you an example. After he suffered his first stroke, he needed an armchair to sit in during the day. Stasya would not buy it for him, even though she was working as a doctor in Beith Lid and, I assume, was earning a reasonable salary. I had no alternative but to go and buy a comfortable armchair for him for eighty Israeli liras out of the money I had saved for the next year of my university studies. Bear in mind that at that time, Stasya had already made him marry her to secure her financial future through the inheritance that was to be boosted by the imminent substantial German restitution, mentioned earlier.

As Lisa would have said to me now, in retrospect, if she could read and summarise this ugly chapter: "*Nice people we had to deal with, Tommy!*" Mind you, Lisa never tried to influence me one way or the other with regard to my dealings with the 'family'. Besides, there were no dealings—all my actions were prompt, swift, and irrevocable. I could never tolerate injustice.

In conclusion to this unhappy chapter, I feel that maybe I should be less critical about my stepfather or father, whoever he may have been. I do not have any conclusive, firm evidence either way about my relationship to him. I only know what I feel based partially on the superficial evidence that I do have. I must admit that I prefer to think of him as my stepfather. The fact that he was German, whereas I grew up being Russian, also contributed to that feeling. This is the way I feel, and this is the way it will remain. Thank you, dear God, for guiding me to this conclusion.

As you may recall, in chapter 5, I was critical of my stepfather because of his coldness— for not telling me anything about himself and his past life and for not taking any interest in what I was doing and feeling as a child: my school and my studies; my difficult uni studies combined with work; my friendships and whatever else was happening in my life. But now, in retrospect, I believe that he may deserve some understanding if, in fact, he too had a bad childhood and life, which turned him into the introverted, negative, inconsiderate person he was to everybody around him.

I believe that difficult life experiences have different effects on different people. I am happy and proud to say that in my case, and even more so in Lisa's case, our bad childhoods and difficult lives that followed made us into better people and better parents.

Contrary to my feelings regarding my stepfather, in the case of my half-sister, I certainly cannot forgive her for her instigated, orchestrated intrigues. She tried to break Lisa and me up twice—before and after our marriage—with her greedy financial objectives in mind. About this I have no doubt whatsoever. I was always a loyal and supportive brother to her in everything. She never criticized Lisa to me, nor would she be able to do so, considering the lovely and kind person that Lisa has always been. Marfa's unexpected betrayal of me can only be attributed to a deep-seated flaw in her character.

In spite of my feelings towards my half-sister, let me say that I am most certainly not a person who does not give people the benefit of doubt or who tends to hold grudges. The very opposite is true! In fact, in the factory where I worked in Israel, amongst a close circle of four friends, I was nicknamed *"Tuvia ha-salchan,"* meaning "Tuvia the forgiver," which I assume is a reference to some biblical story. I was given that nickname after I kept my friendship and asked no questions of a friend who failed to support me at a crucial time in my fight against a bad general manager, thereby leaving me no option but to resign from my position of chief engineer to register my protest. Shortly after my resignation, the GM got the sack.

Chapter 15

Lisa—From Eindhoven, Danzig, Shanghai, Vienna, to Nathanya

My dear, beloved wife, Lisa Nana Dju, was born on February 25, 1933 in Eindhoven, Holland. Her mother, nee Valesca Fischer, was Austrian Jewish, born in 1897 in Perchtoldsdorf, just fifteen kilometres from the centre of Vienna. When all of us travelled together to Europe, we visited Perchtolsdorf and had lunch there.

Lisa's father, Darlee Tshuna Dju, was Chinese, born in Tsing-tien, Chekiang, close to Shanghai. Soon after Lisa's birth, the family moved from Eindhoven to Danzig, which was still a *Freie Stadt* (free city) at that time. (See photo of Lisa and her parents in Danzig.) After World War II, Danzig was returned to Poland and renamed Gdansk. It is now a Polish port. Gdansk is located on the southern coast of the Baltic Sea.

In 1939, just before the outbreak of World War II, Lisa's father converted to Judaism, and the family fled from Nazi-occupied Danzig to Shanghai. In Shanghai, the family lived on Avenue Joffre, in what was then the French Concession, and Lisa attended the American Jewish school.

In 1946, one year after the war ended and after the separation of Lisa's parents, Lisa and her mother returned to Vienna, where they lived on the second floor of a very beautiful, old Vienna building on the Doktor-Karl-Lueger-Platz in the First District, opposite the famous *Stadtpark*. When we were in Vienna together for the last time, we went up to the apartment where Lisa lived after the war and asked the tenants for permission to look at the place, after explaining that we were tourists from Australia and that Lisa used to live there with her mother after the war. They were intrigued by our unusual request and graciously allowed us to walk through their home.

In 1948, after the State of Israel was proclaimed, Lisa and her mother immigrated to Israel and settled in a small township adjacent to the coastal town of Nathanya. Lisa attended the school in Nathanya, which was a difficult time for her because of the new language. In 1952, Lisa was conscripted to compulsory military service, and in May of that year, whilst she was still in boot camp, we met in the camp cinema, as described in an earlier chapter.

After our marriage in 1955 and after I finished my studies in Haifa, Lisa and I settled in Nathanya in 1956, where we rented a room on Herzl Street, on the fifth floor (without a lift) above the Yagil cinema. It was a very nice, sunny room at the corner of the building, which gave it windows on two sides, as well as a small balcony (see photos). The shared bathroom for all the rooms on that floor was at the end of a long corridor. We were young, content with the improvement in our lives, and happy in love.

Whilst living in Nathanya, Lisa travelled to Tel Aviv to study typing and shorthand. In 1957, after we had moved to Tel Aviv, Lisa found a good job with a tourism company, Sightseeing Ltd., on Hayarkon Street, one block away from the Tel Aviv beach. Apart from her secretarial work for the two directors, Lisa took all the bookings from customers, primarily tourists, and organised all the daily bus tours for the fleet of large and mini-buses owned by the company, as well as all plane tours to Eilat and other places. (See two photos that follow of Lisa at her desk.)

In 1960, Lisa left Sightseeing Ltd. to join me for my six-month engineering assignment in Birmingham, England. Upon our return to Tel Aviv, she rejoined Sightseeing Ltd. Lisa worked there right until the birth of our daughter, Iris, in August 1961.

Whilst Lisa was still in hospital after the birth, one of the two Canadian owner-directors of Sightseeing Ltd., Mr. Goldberg, visited her and asked her to return to work, which she had to politely decline. Our baby daughter took precedence.

Lisa was admired and respected by all her coworkers for her conscientious work and her kind and helpful ways with them and customers alike. (See the attached glowing letter of reference from the two Canadian directors.)

Whilst Lisa was working at Sightseeing Ltd., I was able to take several free flights in Dakota DC2 planes to Sdom (Sodom) and see the salt-saturated Dead Sea. The lake is called the Dead Sea because no life can survive in the high salinity of its 1.24 kg/L water. This high-density water enables one to float motionless, instead of swimming in it.

I also flew to Eilat at the southern tip of Israel and the northern end of the Red Sea, adjacent to Jordan and Egypt, and within sight of Saudi Arabia—an interesting place that I would otherwise not have had the opportunity to visit.

Danzig – 1939   Shanghai 1945

Holland 1935

Israel army 1952-54   Tel Aviv, Sightseeing Ltd 1958

Nathanya 1956

Tel Aviv 1957

Nathanya 1956

Tel Aviv, Sightseeing Ltd 1959

Tony Barber Quiz Show 1973

Nathanya 1956

Chapter 16

Post-Graduate Degree—
The End of a Hard Road

After I finished my last semester and the final exams in 1956, I was approached by Chaim, the technical manager of the factory where I worked during the summer breaks as a toolmaker and gear cutter. He offered me the position of design engineer, and I accepted. (Sorry, I was advised not to mention names of companies and people.)

Chaim was born in Poland. He changed his name to an Israeli name to start a new life. He was in his mid-thirties but did not know his date and year of birth after surviving Auschwitz as a child and losing both his parents there. He and his family lived in Holon. He had a small, old Fiat car. In those days, owning any car was considered to be the absolute height of luxury. Every morning, he picked me up in this "limousine" and I rushed down the five flights of stairs to drive with him all the way to the factory, which was just over half an hour away.

The Technion assigned to me the post-graduate project of automotive aluminium piston production, which I managed to do after work and on Saturdays (the only day off work). It took me over a year to complete this project. Lisa helped me with some of the standard gauge drawings. In 1957, Lisa and I moved from Nathanya to a three-room apartment at 22 Amsterdam Street in Tel Aviv, which enabled Lisa to find a good secretarial position in Tel Aviv and also reduced my travelling time to and from work by bus 22. (Twenty-two was to become our lucky number).

Our apartment was on the ground floor, and the third empty room was soon taken over by a group of stray cats that accessed it through the open window for breakfast and dinner. The following year, one of the cats, named Mauli by Lisa, passed away in the cellar of the building, with the decaying corpse creating an unbearable sweet, rotting smell. We had to call the landlord, who managed with some difficulty to remove it.

Upon completion of my post-graduate project, I submitted it to the panel of lecturers and professors at the Technion. After they had reviewed it, I had to face them and answer questions about the piston product design, dimensioning and tolerancing, my specified sequence of manufacturing operations, production equipment used and the design of my machining fixtures and gauges. All this was relatively easy for me, and I received my Bachelor of Science degree in mechanical engineering and post-graduate degree of Dipl. Ing. (Diplom Ingenieur) with honours.

This was the successful end of a truly hard road to professional engineering, combining work with studies, in a difficult foreign language. I did not attend the graduation ceremony, just as I did not attend my high school certificate-presentation ceremony in Harbin. I'm nothing if not consistent! As you will see in a later chapter, our daughter, Iris, will inherit my introverted attitude for such occasions.

Thanks to Lisa's cooking, our improved financial situation, reduced stress, and my regular meals, I gained a lot of weight, reaching a maximum of eighty-four kilos. (See photo of Lisa and me that follows.) This was a very happy, relaxed time for Lisa and me, as well as a very satisfying start in my professional career as design engineer with no managerial responsibilities.

Chapter 17

Engineering—Interesting Start in Design

My years at the factory from 1956 to 1960 were good, constructive years. I managed to do a lot of exceptionally good engineering work, drawing up a wide range of parts and assemblies, specifying manufacturing tolerances, steel specifications, and heat treatments, and designing a variety of very complex cutting tools, such as gear-cutting hobs, large straight and spiral broaches. I was assisted in my design by excellent Russian engineering books on this subject. Under normal circumstances, these types of complex cutting tools would be purchased from companies that specialise in their design and manufacture, but there were no such companies in Israel in those years. Importing these tools was difficult and expensive, requiring unfavourable foreign-exchange payment, so we had to improvise. As you can imagine, I did not just improvise—my complex cutting tools were perfect.

I also managed to upgrade the machine that we needed to manufacture these complex cutting tools and was able to come up with the calculations to achieve the necessary reciprocal spiral undercutting movements, because our very old Reineke machine had never been used by the company before and had no operating manual. When producing the hob on such a special lathe, the cutting tool has to move in and out of the work piece at each intersection of two spirals, in order to create the clearance angle on each of the hob's teeth. (Laurochka, I have gone into just a wee bit of detail in case your partner or son turns out to be a mechanical engineer, like your grandfather.)

In 1958, I was promoted to head of the Engineering Department. Together with the technical manager, Chaim; the production manager, Moshe; and the tool room manager, Yitzchak, we formed a very strong team and managed to transform the company into a progressive, highly skilled manufacturing unit.

Moshe was in his mid-thirties, born in Israel; he was almost completely bald and used to say, "Instead of a comb, I now use a towel." He had plenty of energy, rushing around the factory, solving problems, and "extinguishing fires" wherever they occurred. He was also a musician, playing the accordion at various functions after work. He was often chosen as the perfect scapegoat by the general manager when things went wrong. The stress at work affected his health, and his doctor advised him to record it all in a diary to get it off his chest and his mind. He followed that advice, and it worked.

Yitzchak, also born in Poland, was about thirty years old, highly intelligent, and a brilliant toolmaker. He was a good, fair-minded person, who would not get involved in company politics. During his military service, he was a sergeant on a submarine in the Red Sea.

Our technical success did not go unnoticed by a much larger company in the same market but without our manufacturing skills. As a result, our factory was taken over by that company. Unfortunately, the choice of general managers for our factory resulted in one bad general manager after another.

In 1959, another GM was appointed to manage our company. He was a mean, aggressive fellow, treating people without due respect. My position in the company was very strong, and he was fully aware of it. On a number of occasions, when he displayed his arrogance towards workers on the factory floor, I stepped in to their defence and, by doing so, embarrassed him in front of those people. On one such occasion, as he and I were walking away from the scene of his embarrassment, he turned to me and in a pleading voice asked me to please not say these things to him in front of other people. However, as time went on, he could not help being himself, and nor could I. During stop-work meetings and strikes, I joined the workers in their demonstrations in front of the factory building. Joining the factory workers' strike action was not a normally accepted position for a senior manager such as the head of the Engineering Department.

I was not happy with what was happening to the company and its employees under this general management and registered my protest by handing in my resignation. When the business owner happened to visit the factory, he was hoping I would approach him with my grievances, but this was never my intention. I was young and stubborn, not prepared to negotiate and make compromises.

During the farewell party, I received many presents from my team and all my many other friends in the factory, including an expensive briefcase, a complete top-brand drafting set, a complete range of Rapidograph drafting pens for different line thicknesses, and many other things. The GM would definitely not have been welcome at that party!

Chapter 18

Our First Real Estate—From Humble Beginnings

In 1958, we bought a small but brand-new 1½-room apartment with a long balcony on the third floor of 23 Alexander Yanai Street in Tsafon Tel Aviv (North Tel Aviv, which was the new, modern part of the city). In Israel, we counted the number of rooms, rather that the number of bedrooms, as we do in Australia. Lisa and I occupied the larger room, and Lisa's mother, Vally, occupied the smaller one, referred to as a half-room. There was also a small hallway and a dining area outside the kitchen. The balcony extended the full length of the apartment, starting with our room, past the bathroom and kitchen, and ending with Vally's room. It suited our requirements, and it was something we could afford financially. Our apartment was directly below the flat roof. The roof was accessible, and Lisa used it during her pregnancy for her daily walks. After Iris was born, her crib was accommodated in our room, as well as my desk and drawing board.

When we took in a stray cat, we cut out the bottom corner of our front door to provide convenient access for our feline friend.

Many things that Lisa and I experienced over the years involved the number twenty-two. The street number twenty-three on Alexander Yanai Street surprised us, until we walked around the corner and found that our building was numbered twenty-two on Horkanus Street. Lisa got married at the age of twenty-two; I served in Armed Forces Unit 22; we lived in Tel Aviv at Amsterdam Street 22, whilst I was taking bus number twenty-two to work; and then we bought our small apartment at 22 Horkanus Street. I met my mother twenty-two years after we were separated by the Nazis. I worked together with my chief design draftsman, David, for twenty-two years. Many twenty-twos followed in our life in Australia, including our current Sydney postcode, 2022. When returning from my frequent overseas business trips, I used to bring Lisa a small bottle of her favourite Chanel #22 perfume.

Twenty-two proved to be our lucky number throughout our happy life together, except when in 2009, Lisa stayed at the Wolper Hospital for twenty-two days and passed away in Room 1022. I hope that Lisa took the number twenty-two with her and made it a lucky number once again in her new life and for us both to share again when I join her.

After my resignation, whilst I was still looking for a new position, Moshe and Yitzchak used to visit us every day after work at our new home in Alexander Yanai. We sat together on our balcony, where Lisa served us dinner. Moshe and Yitzchak reported to me the daily events at the factory, which included the dismissal of the GM soon after my resignation.

I went for a job interview at the Weizmann Institute of Science, located in Rechovot, an international centre of scientific research. The person who interviewed me, responsible for Research & Development of new products, was looking for an engineer to develop new high-quality loudspeakers. The interview started by him asking me to draw a tree. That was easy for me. I started by drawing the base of the tree with large, strong roots spreading far to the sides and deep down into the ground. Only then did I draw the trunk, branches, etc. He was visibly impressed by what I had done. In retrospect, it is easy for me to understand why he was impressed, but this only occurred to me later.

Unfortunately, when I rang the institute a week or two later, I was told that the advertised position was no longer considered by the institute because the head of Research & Development who interviewed me had passed away—he drowned. Had this tragic death not occurred, I believe that I would still be working at the Weizmann Institute today. I read that Israel's Weizmann Institute is considered to be one of the best places in the world for academics to work.

I must add this interesting comment from my good friend, psychologist Dr. Sarah Edelman, about my experience with the Weizmann Institute. She wrote, "That's very interesting—a strange quirk of fate, sometimes referred to as 'sliding doors'—where life may have taken us in a different direction if something had or had not happened."

It seems to me that there would have been many such "sliding-doors" situations of varying magnitude in many lives, especially in the lives of people during the turbulent thirties and forties of the last century all across Europe and Asia, from Spain and central Europe in the west and all the way across the USSR and China in the east.

This also reminds me of two earlier major sliding-doors situations in my own life. The first one happened when my stepfather was waiting for his patient, the Argentinean consul, to issue our visas to emigrate and settle in Argentina, which, unbeknownst to him, was thwarted by my mother. It became too late to remedy this situation, and instead we fled to China. I have no regrets about this because I am much happier to have grown up in a Russian community than in a Latin American one. Besides, I would not have met Lisa, and Iris and Laura would not have been born.

The second sliding-doors situation happened in Harbin, when Helmut Stern had the crazy, unrealistic plan of writing to the newly established Israeli Embassy in Moscow, asking for visas to Israel, ignoring the fact that his letter and the embassy's reply would have to somehow be able to pass both the Chinese and Soviet censorship—not just once but twice. Nevertheless, he proved everybody wrong, and so I ended up in Israel and the free world, instead of the Soviet Union. Most of my schoolmates must have ended up in the USSR. Conclusion: contrary to what rational thinking may predict with high probability, fate will often prevail, making the impossible possible. In Russia, the belief in fate is traditionally very strong.

I would like to examine my above-mentioned tree drawing at the Weizmann Institute in a bit more detail. It was undoubtedly a psychological/psychotechnical test given to me by the head of R & D, to test my thoroughness, reliability, and detail-minded stable attitude to engineering R & D work. Although I was a good drawer from early childhood and always drew trees this way, it seems to me that these large, spreading roots signified my desire for stability in my life, reflecting my childhood frustration for not having had a stable, loving family and my wish for a reliable, permanent belonging, described in the introduction chapter.

Getting back to my job-seeking situation, I eventually joined an aviation factory as assistant chief manufacturing engineer. I was unhappy there, mainly because of, in my opinion, the simplistic system of manufacturing tolerancing, which appears to be normal practice in small-batch production in some aviation industries, compared to what was normal practice for me in mass production of other industries, required to achieve reliable interchangeability in assembly. I proved my point to management by analysing a plane's undercarriage part and assembly drawings. I resigned from my position after just four months of working there.

When I explained the reasons for my resignation to the GM, I mentioned my concern about these production specifications, as well as my unfortunate lack of interest in aviation production, adding that all planes looked alike and were complete *"mystères"* to me. (The Mystère was a French fighter-bomber plane in those days.)

The second and main reason for my resignation was that the owner and the senior management at head office wanted me back in my previous job. I received an offer from them that I could not refuse. More details follow in the next chapter.

Chapter 19

Back Where I Belong—My Professional Success

As already mentioned before, soon after my resignation, the GM had to leave. The company wanted me back. Because of my experience in gear design and manufacture, as well as to entice me to come back, I was offered a six-month stay in the UK to study the design and manufacture of Gleason Hypoid gears. I accepted their offer.

I had to visit the head office, where the new owner and senior management were located, and sign an agreement, committing myself to stay with the company for five years after my return from the UK. Should I fail to complete this full term of service, I would have to repay the corresponding proportion of all costs of travel, accommodation, and living expenses in the UK. I doubt whether such a commitment would be legal under our present industrial laws, however, it seems to have been legal then and there.

And so, in 1960, I flew to London with KLM Airlines, my first flight in a jet-engine plane. I took with me one suitcase of personal belongings and another suitcase full of books on gear design and manufacture. It was so heavy that the assistant GM, who saw me off at Lod Airport, asked me if all these books were really essential—and then paid for them as overweight luggage. In those days, international flights were a big deal.

Lisa watched the plane take off and got worried when she saw the trail of dark exhaust fumes from the plane's jet engines, but Itzchak calmed her down, explaining that this was normal for these jet planes when you observe them from a tail-end position, which increases the depth of the smoke tail.

Lisa took time off from her position at Sightseeing and followed me by sea and land at our own expense, together with her mother, Vally, because air travel was quite expensive in those years.

I forgot to mention in previous chapters that Vally lived with us wherever we lived and travelled with us wherever we travelled, including Australia and all our overseas trips from Australia to Europe and Hawaii. Nevertheless, she always complained to us and to all our neighbours that we were about to either leave her behind or ask her to leave home—and no assurances from Lisa and me, verbally and in writing, would succeed in depriving her of this pleasure. I only had to put up with this nonsense since our marriage. In spite of being a most caring, conscientious, and responsible daughter, Lisa had to endure this and other ongoing mental torture since early childhood. I went along with it because, had I retaliated to Vally's behaviour, it would have rebounded on Lisa. We had no alternative but to take care of Vally, and she realised this and took full advantage of it. It seems to me that this completely unwarranted insecurity on Vally's part may have been a result of some childhood problems, and her two failed marriages, first to Dr. Alexandrovich and then to Darlee Tshuna Dju.

The new owner of the business decided to expand our manufacturing facilities and build a brand-new large factory. A know-how agreement was signed with a group of companies in the UK (sorry, no names), and I was able to spend time at one of their subsidiaries in Birmingham, where gears were being produced for most of the UK industry. I was also able to visit another subsidiary where they produced some other components. We were already doing part of this work ourselves, but on a much smaller scale.

During my six months in the UK, I travelled to many different, very interesting places. I loved visiting old, established English factories, with all their know-how and industrial tradition, with most of them located close to small townships amidst the beautiful English countryside. I also enjoyed the old English country hotels, like the White Horse Hotel in Huddersfield. I cannot remember the names of all the places in the UK that I visited to gather information on manufacturing technologies and to obtain quotations for equipment and tooling. Here are just a few of them: David Brown in Huddersfield, Sykes in Staines, Ford in Dagenham, Red Ring in Coventry, Avery, etc. Sorry, these are all the names I can remember—fifty-four years have passed since then!

One unforgettable experience happened when I was returning from Huddersfield, where I visited two companies, the David Brown gear cutting-tool factory and the David Brown tractor factory. Rather than staying another night at the White Horse Hotel in Huddersfield, I decided to travel back by train to Birmingham, where we lived in a rented home. Leaving Huddersfield late in the evening meant that there were no direct trains to Birmingham. I had to change trains at Stoke-on-Trent and wait for the connecting train for about two hours, at some time past midnight. Rather than sit at the train station, I went to explore Stoke. Being a small town, there were only a few streetlights; however, the totally deserted streets were lit by a full moon. It was as though this whole scene, including the stream that ran through the town, was created by Hollywood for me alone. The only sounds were those created by that stream and my footsteps. It was truly a magical experience.

Being overseas guests, my Indian friend, Gurudas Kopikar, and I shared all our lunches with senior executives in their exclusive dining room. Very British indeed! In spite of the generally poor reputation of the English cuisine in those days, the food was excellent, served elegantly on beautiful china with sparkling silver on immaculate white tablecloths. The chef was an interesting character who could have easily made a career in Hollywood as a typical English sergeant major, which he was in his younger years. He still had his sergeant major's posture and bearing, moustache, and demeanour. He entertained all of us, his captive audience at lunch, by standing amongst the tables and relating in a loud voice for everyone to hear his humorous stories from army experience and life in general.

Gurudas Kopikar was an engineer from Mahindra-Mahindra in India, on a similar mission to mine. His girlfriend was a blonde German girl, whom he later married. About thirty-five years later, whilst visiting a stand of an Indian company at an engineering exhibition in Sydney, I mentioned to the engineer on that stand that back in 1960, I knew an engineer by the name of Gurudas Kopikar, to which he responded nonchalantly, "Oh yes, I know him," and proceeded to tell me that Gurudas eventually joined his father-in-law's textile factory in Germany. A small world, considering that, prior to Gurudas moving to Germany, there were already a billion people in India, with a cool few million mechanical engineers amongst them!

That's enough about work. Let me tell you a bit about Lisa's and my private life in Birmingham, as well as our visit to London, where we met my mother and her German husband, Erich Otto.

We rented three rooms in a nice, old English home in the Birmingham suburb of Mosely Village. The elderly owners, Mrs. Gaye Phillips and her husband, were friendly, gentle people. They lived on the ground floor, and our rooms were on the first floor. Gaye liked to putter in her long back garden. I cannot remember during which months of the year we were there, but considering the fact that the weather was pretty good throughout our six-month stay in the UK, we must have been there from about April to September. It was in the UK that we first watched TV, naturally black-and-white. The programs that Lisa and I remembered are *Rawhide,* with Clint Eastwood as Rowdy; *Bonanza,* with Lorne Greene, Adam, Hoss, and Little Joe; *Hancock's Half Hour,* with Tony Hancock and Sid James; *Sunday Night at the London Palladium,* with such stars as Nat King Cole and the ever-young Cliff Richards, who was truly young at that time; *Armchair Mystery,* with Donald Pleasance; and *Hitchcock Mysteries.* Lisa provided me with all these names, because with my poor memory for names, I would not have been able to come up with that list. We also remembered the tunes and rhymes of some of the British commercials, such as Wall's Ice Cream, sliding Mr. Sheen and, of course, Watkins beer, even though we did not drink any.

On weekends, which were the first two-day-weekends we had ever experienced (in Israel, it was just one day), we used to go walking in Cannon Hill Park and the woods of Lickey Hills.

We also liked to have dinner at the Chinese restaurant close to the railway station. There we could order half-portions, and in doing so, sample more dishes. We enjoyed the Chinese food, because in Israel, we missed it. There were no Chinese restaurants in those years.

To the best of our knowledge, there were also no Chinese people residing in Israel at that time except, I assume, for diplomatic staff in the capital, Jerusalem. This made Lisa rather distinctive in Israel, and I was the lucky one to snare her. How about that? I only had two loves in my life, and both of them were half-Chinese. Laura, should you have a son or sons, please pass on my unreserved strong recommendation for a similar choice to be made by them. I am serious!

I was given an allowance of five pounds, five shillings—five guineas a day—which was a very generous amount in 1960. It was more than enough for all our living expenses and rent, leaving plenty for Lisa's clothes shopping for herself and for me at her favourite Marks & Spencer store, even though, like most men, I have never been too keen on new clothes.

Chapter 20

Meeting My Mother—After Twenty-Two Years; London and Paris

As you will recall, the Shanghai barkeeper whom I met on the SS *Wooster Victory* on the way to Haifa helped me to locate my mother in Berlin. Ten years had passed since I was able to locate her in Berlin in 1950, but we had not yet met. She lived in Germany, and she knew that I was not prepared to travel to Germany. I suppose we could have met during those ten years in some other European country, but as far as I can remember, this possibility had never been discussed. In any case, I could not have travelled during the two years of my military service. After my discharge from the air force, I was too busy either working to earn money for my studies or else studying in Haifa. So now that Lisa and I were in the UK, the perfect opportunity presented itself for us to meet in London, when I was close to completing my work in the UK, and for all of us to travel together to Paris for another short holiday.

We met my mother and her husband, Erich Otto, upon their arrival at Heathrow Airport. Strangely, I cannot remember much detail of that initial meeting. Obviously, it was a very important meeting, and yet I seem to have some mental block about it. It must have been a rather emotional experience for my mother, although she was not one to show it. For me, it would have been a somewhat stressful experience, because being a grown man of twenty-eight years old, and after a twenty-two-year-long separation from my mother, I was no longer capable of feeling what should have been a normal mother-son relationship—definitely my fault. It would have required more than just those few days that we were able to spend together, for a normal relationship to be restored, especially bearing in mind that even in my early childhood, we were not able to spend much time together. Sadly, it was an abnormal situation in an ongoing abnormal relationship. And yet, to this day, I still love and miss my mother—even more so than back than in London.

We all stayed a few days together in London at the Strand Hotel. We did some sightseeing together. At the end of this chapter is a photo of the four of us outside the main gate to Buckingham Palace. I also remember the little park outside the palace with a long artificial pond and many white ducks in and around it. (In keeping with the times, coloured ones may have been discriminated against and excluded. I also carried some of this particular experience back to the hotel under the soles of my shoes.) After a few days, we had to travel back to Birmingham because I had some business to complete. We then travelled together to Paris by train. In the middle of the night, whilst we were all fast asleep, the train crossed the channel by driving onto and off a ferry; it then proceeded again on land to its destination in Paris. There was no underwater tunnel yet in those days. In Paris, we booked into the St. James Hotel on the Rue St. Honoré. That evening, we all had dinner at a restaurant in the Rue de Rivoli where, amongst other things, we were served artichokes, previously unknown to Lisa and me, and also unknown to my worldly mother and her husband—so we had to ask the waiter how to eat them.

I do not remember which Paris sites we may have visited together with my mother and Erich. Only years later, Lisa, Iris, and I visited all the amazing, beautiful places in Paris, with the Musée d'Orsay being one of our absolute favourites, especially when visiting there first thing in the morning, before the crowds gathered. A few years later, Iris and Laura travelled on their own to Paris, Rome, and Venice, visiting many art galleries and taking pictures of many statues, which, upon coming home, Iris captured most beautifully on canvas in pastel. You can see one of these wonderful paintings on a page that follows, but only in black and white.

To see Iris's art in colour, please visit her website *http://iristoren.com* . What impresses me most in her portraits is her ability to capture not only the resemblance but also the facial expressions and mood of her subjects, both in grown-ups and children. This, I believe, is what makes her portraits perfect. She is happy to accept commissions for portraits, still life, landscapes, and sketches. She is happy to accept portrait commissions from photos with a payment-on-approval basis.

Iris was a student of the prestigious Julian Ashton Art School in Sydney, where she obtained her diplomas in drawing and painting and received the Henry Gibbons Art Prize in 1984.

Back to my other favourite professional painter, my mother. We parted with my mother and Erich in Paris. In the years to come, after settling in Sydney, I visited them regularly during my engineering business trips to Europe. By then, they had moved from Berlin to Wiesbaden, before or after the Soviet blockade of Berlin, and then to a small town called Hiddessen, near Bielefeld, not too far from Hannover. I got to know both of them much better. Erich Otto was a very decent person who suffered under the Nazis. Being a classical theatre actor, he lost his work permit and became dependent on my mother during the Nazi years. After the war, he was reinstated to become head of the theatre actors' union once again, during which time he helped his persecuted friends, both Jewish and Christian, to obtain restitution money from the German government. Erich also successfully managed my restitution claim for interrupted schooling. I cannot remember how much money it amounted to—it may have been just around DM 10,000. It was a modest amount but nevertheless a welcome injection of cash for our monthly repayments of two mortgages.

From Paris, my mother and Erich returned to Germany, whilst Lisa, Vally, and I travelled to Marseilles. There we boarded a Turkish ship by the name of *Istanbul* and set sail for Haifa. We had a brief stopover in Napoli where, after an inspection of the city and its famous Castel Nuovo from a distance, which still has a spherical cannonball embedded in its bronze gate, and after buying a bottle of Chianti wine within a woven basket, we boarded the ship and proceeded to Haifa. This whole journey took just four days, during which time I overdosed on aspirin tablets, trying to get rid of my migraine headache. The ship's doctor did not seem to be able to help me. After disembarking in Haifa, we were met by our friends, Yitzchak and Moshe, and driven to our home in Tel Aviv.

Whenever I visited my mother and Erich in Hiddessen for a day or two, I slept on the sofa in the lounge. When washing my hands, I used water sparingly—the Israeli way. If my mother saw me do so, she would march into the bathroom with a serious expression on her face and turn the tap on for a decent flow of water and march out. This type of silent action was typical of her.

She also liked to relate and demonstrate the way she dealt with her Nazi brother-in-law, who became an officer in the German army. Being fluent in Russian and Polish, he would have no doubt distinguished himself on the Eastern Front, if you know what I mean—he would have been responsible for the loss of many innocent civilian lives. During the war, he once came to my mother unannounced for some unknown and never-identified reason. No sooner had he entered her apartment than she went back to the front door, holding it open with one hand and pointing the way out with her other hand—needless to say, without saying a word. I hope he had a becoming end, especially if the Russians captured him.

Erich was hard of hearing and therefore tended to speak in a loud voice. When he and my mother used to retire to their bedroom after dinner, I could not help overhearing some of what they were saying. On one such occasion, my mother must have said something to Erich about my lack of affection, to which he replied, "Well, he is a grown-up man and does not need a mother anymore." *(Aber er ist doch ein erwachsener Mann und braucht keine Mutter mehr.)* I am sure that he did not mean to hurt my mother. Nevertheless, I cannot imagine that this was what my mother wanted to hear. In retrospect, I feel sorry for having been so cold to her.

Erich had lost his daughter from his first marriage as a result of Nazi persecution. I do not know the exact details, except that being his daughter, she was refused medical attention. Erich passed away in 1977, when he was in his nineties. My mother passed away the following year when she was eighty-five years old. I spoke on the phone to her doctor in hospital, who informed me that she had bowel cancer. I suggested to him not to tell her of her terminal sickness, because this would not have served any positive purpose; it would only have added mental stress to her physical suffering.

I flew to Frankfurt, then to Düsseldorf, and then travelled by train to Bielefeld, and finally by taxi to Hiddessen to attend her funeral. My mother's neighbours, the Bierbaum couple, were very helpful to my mother before her death and to me during my last visit there. She was buried in the small cemetery of Hiddessen, close to Erich's grave, after a brief civil service. May they both rest in peace. I do hope that we meet again; there is so much I must tell my mother, and there are so many questions I would like to ask her!

My mother and Erich "chose" to be born and live in the wrong centuries (nineteenth and twentieth) with the First and Second World Wars and throughout the Nazi years. My timing was not too good either. Most importantly, I hope and pray that this twenty-first century turns out to be good for Iris and Laura, as well as for Laura's children and grandchildren. Please, dear God!

I assume that my mother's choice for a civil-service funeral was because of her strong dislike of the Church. She was very outspoken about it. I further assume that this dislike was due to the fact that the Church did not stand up against the Nazi regime; that she was separated from her children because of the Nazis; that her Jewish partner was executed by the Nazis; and for Erich's years of suffering.

Because of my short visit to Hiddessen, the same Qantas cabin crew that took me to Frankfurt also returned me home to Sydney two days later.

I left all of my mother's furniture to her neighbours in gratitude for their generous help. My mother left them DM 10,000. The major share of money she left to us, Lisa and me. Because of my rushed visit, I failed to bring home a beautiful oil painting by my mother—a portrait of a little girl and a small bird sitting on the girl's finger. I should have also brought home a lovely carved wooden statue of the Madonna, which I assume was made in the image of the famous Black Madonna for which Czestochowa is famous. As you will recall, Czestochowa was where my mother was born and educated.

Mother at home in Berlin

My mother and Erich with us
in London and Paris – 1960

Beer Sheva 1958
(the camels also appear to be in love)

1961 – our new apartment
1962 – we had to sell it and leave Israel!

Chapter 21

Birth of Our Daughter, Iris—Happiness!

Lisa and I had been married for five years when, late in 1960, after our return from the UK, we decided the time was right for Lisa to have a baby. We now had a home of our own, and I had a steady position and income—or so we thought, not expecting what was going to happen just two years later.

Lisa was able to conceive straight away and went for regular checkups to the obstetrician, Dr. Fuchs. I often joined Lisa during her evening exercise walks on the flat roof of our building. (All rooves in Israel are flat—I assume to be able to catch rainwater, if need be.) Ultrasound examinations of babies in the womb were not yet available. When the time came on the evening of August 12, 1961 to go to the Assuta Hospital, Israel's largest private hospital, I drove Lisa there in our company Jeep CJ5.

Lisa's labour was natural, relatively easy, and not lasting very long (with the emphasis on the word *relatively*). Iris was born late that evening. It was not yet the accepted practice for husbands to stay with their wives during labour. I first saw Iris through the long window separating the dads from their babies. Needless to say, Iris was the most beautiful, healthiest baby of the lot. She had a bit of jaundice, which apparently is not uncommon. This gave the baby a beautiful peachy colour. I think Lisa and Iris stayed in hospital for just two days. I drove them home—yes, those were happy days! A few days later, I went to the government office, which was not far away from where we lived, to register Iris's birth as daughter of Alisa and Tuvia Toren. We had already changed our surname to Toren in 1957, whilst still in Nathanya. *Toren* in Hebrew means *mast,* like a ship's mast. *Торин* is also a Russian surname with the typical "*in*" ending.

Before little Iris was born, my mother sent us a beautiful pram, blanket, and linen. When Lisa went to pick it up from Customs, the official looked at her advanced stage of pregnancy and did not charge her any custom duty.

Iris's crib was in our bedroom, which also served as our lounge room and my study. A paediatrician lady used to come to us regularly to check on Iris's progress. On one occasion, whilst little Iris was lying on my desk and the doctor was examining her, she suddenly let go of a tall stream, narrowly missing the doctor. We all burst out laughing. (In contrast to that paediatrician lady, when thirty-two years later, Iris's daughter, Laura, was born in Sydney, we were surprised to find that all the paediatricians in our area were males. This does not make any sense to me. Generally speaking, male paediatricians could not possibly be as good as female paediatricians. The male doctors/specialists must be intentionally blocking female medical graduates from specialising in this field of medicine because they are justifiably afraid of female competition.)

When we moved to our new three-room apartment the following year, Iris had her own nursery room. It was a particularly nice room with plenty of light. It was beautifully furnished—the tall chest of drawers had pink doors and beige sides, with many toys on top, including the dolls, Jimmy and Boyly.

A year later, when Iris was just sixteen months old, the unforseen happened—we had to sell our lovely new home and leave Israel for Australia. Find out why in the next two chapters.

Iris – 2 months old

Iris – 2 ½ years old

Iris – 8 months old

Chapter 22

Our New Home—Difficult Decisions

Soon after our return from the UK to Tel Aviv, the new factory construction was completed, and all the machines and the Heat-Treatment Department were transferred and installed in this very large, modern factory. New machines for cutting, lapping, and testing of gears, including Fellows gear-shaping and Maag gear-grinding machines were also installed.

I was again appointed to head of engineering, responsible for twenty-two engineers and draftspersons, some of whom I brought over from the old factory and others I interviewed and engaged when already in our new location. My team included:

- Amy, an ex-air force pilot, a Sabra (i.e., born in Israel), Technion graduate and a very cool character;
- Aaron, also a Sabra and Technion graduate and a bit of a loner;
- Selvin, a Russian-speaking mature Polish engineer and a particularly nice person;
- Steward, an American citizen and engineer, who was imprisoned in the United States during the war for refusing to join the army; not Jewish, but came to Israel as an idealist—also a particularly nice, peaceful human being;
- Yoshua, an extraordinarily gifted design draftsman, originally from Hungary, a tall, strong, and good-looking diabetic, who died as a young man when we were already in Australia;
- Elieser, nicknamed Junior (which he was no longer), but whose surname I can no longer remember, a diligent, good draftsman, originally from Poland;
- Avraham, a technician from Yugoslavia who was learning gear calculations and design from me;

- Harry, a very good draftsman from Romania, whom I engaged and taught years ago, and a particularly loyal friend;
- Shula, a very quiet, diligent draftswoman;
- Ezra, a Sabra—another draftsman;
- an elderly, retired gentleman, originally from Perth, Australia, who did all our dyeline printing.

After fifty-two years, I could only remember eleven out of twenty-two names. I thought you may be interested in seeing the many nationalities, with only three out of eleven listed being Sabras, born in Israel. A Sabra is the prickly, red desert cactus fruit, which is soft and sweet inside. People born in Israel are compared to the Sabra because they are tough on the outside and sweet on the inside. Our daughter, Iris, is a Sabra, having been born in Israel.

During the first few months, I drove every day from our home in Tel Aviv to the new factory in my company car, picking up my friends, Moshe and Itzchak, on the way in Ramat Gan. This drive took about forty minutes each way. Like many others, we decided to move closer to the factory. We signed a contract with a builder, purchasing a three-room home unit (condominium) from a plan, with two balconies on the second/top floor of a new development site. The rear balcony had an open but distant view of the Mediterranean Sea. By the time the building was completed, we managed to sell our small home unit in Tel Aviv, pay off our two mortgages, and obtain a new mortgage for our new home and settle the purchase. We spent a lot of money furnishing our new place. Lisa and I spent many happy Saturdays at the Shook Ha-Carmel (the Carmel Markets) in Tel Aviv, buying furniture and things for our new home. Whenever we went to the Carmel Markets, we took the opportunity to visit a nearby restaurant on Ben Yehuda Street, where they served the very best bagels ever, never to be repeated anywhere, not even in New York.

We moved to our new home in early 1962, the year the Nazi organiser of the Holocaust, Adolf Eichmann, was found guilty of crimes against humanity and executed by hanging. He was captured by Mossad operatives in Argentina in 1960 and taken to Israel to face trial in an Israeli court. Clemency was denied by Israeli president Yitzhak Ben-Zwi. As far as I can remember, his ashes were scattered at sea to prevent the possibility, however remote, that his remains may get into the wrong hands and be used as part of a Nazi shrine. His evil soul must have gone straight to hell. As you can imagine, there is a lot of information about him on the Internet. I did not feel like reading it; even looking at his photo, his cold, cruel face, was more than enough for me.

The core technical team of Chaim, Moshe, Itzchak, and me, as before in the old factory, was still fully functional. Also as before, another bad general manager was appointed. He was a short, stocky fellow with a thin little moustache, cold light-blue eyes, and an unblinking, arrogant stare that said, "I am very important." His looks reminded me of the king of diamonds in a pack of playing cards. He was all show and no substance. As far as we could judge, he appeared to have no industrial, commercial, manufacturing, or engineering knowledge whatsoever. He transformed the factory into a show ground, with everything neatly stacked away, with freshly painted white lines identifying the traffic lanes between rows of production machines being his only "contribution." He expected his senior staff to be neatly dressed, wearing a business shirt and tie, and most importantly, to be clean-shaven like in his good old days in the army. Well, guess who demonstrably did not comply. He knew—that I knew—that he knew—that there was nothing he could do to make me join him in his silly games. I was too busy with important work.

However, he did try to get back at me once. I was the only person except for him who had a company car. Just before leaving work late on a Friday afternoon, one of the section managers came to me, saying that he had some important personal matters that Saturday and that the GM told him he could have my car. Needless to say, he did not get my car on this or any other occasion.

A few more months of mismanagement followed, and when reckoning day grew close, the GM found himself a scapegoat by firing the technical manager, my friend Chaim. I promptly resigned in solidarity with Chaim.

A few days after my resignation, my whole twenty-two-strong engineering team arrived unannounced at our home to ask me to return to work. I thanked them for their loyalty but explained that this was not an acceptable option for me.

Chapter 23

Leaving Israel—Significant Financial Sacrifices

I resigned after serving only two out of the five years that I was committed to under the contract I had signed prior to going to the UK. I was left with no alternative but to repay 60 percent (three out of five years) of all the expenses associated with my trip, including all travelling fares, hotel accommodations, six months of living expenses, a retired American engineer's return airfare from the United States, and his accommodation in a Birmingham hotel (where he taught me Hypoid gear calculations), and whatever else they could drag up in trying to stop me from leaving.

My mind was made up. I was too young and too stubborn to consider any compromises.

The head office management offered to send me and my family for a two-month vacation to a resort in Cyprus if I was prepared to return to work, which was very generous of them. By then, having lost both his technical manager and his chief engineer, the GM got the sack, but I did not feel like going back anymore. The situation required a clean break. I needed a change. The only solution was to sell our lovely new home and repay my debt—but before doing so, we had to decide what to do next.

Chaim had an uncle living in Caulfield, Melbourne, in faraway Australia, to whom he referred to as "fetter Wervel." Lisa had relatives in Sydney: Ruth and Rafi Widder, Paul and Mia Meyer, and the sisters Elsa and Lily Buckwell. So, both our families decided to immigrate to Australia, and with this in mind, we travelled to Tel Aviv, where the Australian Consulate was located on Hayarkon Street (the same street as Sightseeing Ltd., where Lisa used to work). During the weeks that followed, we filled out all the necessary forms and applied for an immigration visa and permanent residence in

Australia. In addition, I wrote to the Institution of Engineers Australia, submitting my qualification documents and requesting to be accepted as a Certified Professional Engineer and Member of the Institution.

After we and Chaim's family obtained the Australian visas and I was accepted into the Institution of Engineers Australia, Lisa and I proceeded to sell our home to repay our debts.

At this point, the second in command at the head office was sent to negotiate with Chaim and me at our homes, with one of their strategic objectives, I assume, being to include our wives in these negotiations. Chaim and his wife were successfully enticed by the emissary, whereas I refused to meet with him. Therefore, the dice were cast for us, with only one option remaining: that was to immigrate to Oz.

Management had one more trump card to play, but at that stage, they were unaware of it. I had to make sure they did not find out about it and did not get the chance to play it. I believe that, had they known we intended to leave Israel, they would have had no problem whatsoever in stopping me from leaving the country. Unfortunately, I cannot reveal any details, but one phone call to the appropriate authorities, and we would have been kept in Israel, with no solutions that I can think of except going back to work for the company. We were acutely aware of this danger and did not confide in anyone about our immigration plans, not even to my closest friends, Itzchak and Moshe—not because I did not trust them personally, but because a member of their family could have unwittingly passed the information on. Chaim and his wife, Shoshana, were the only ones who, naturally, knew all about it, having planned it together with us and then abandoning their plan.

Yet, there was another person who knew of our plans—Lisa's mother, Vally. She knew because we took her along to the Australian Consulate to apply and receive her visa. Before long, we had another regular domestic crisis, during which she accused us of planning to leave her behind in Israel. To prevent this from happening, she threatened to go to the company management for help and to tell them of our plans and our wickedness towards her. We knew from past experiences that these threats were real, because on many previous occasions, she had gone to friends and neighbours and complained about us. Fortunately, nothing happened, probably because she derived enough satisfaction from frightening us. She would also have been looking forward to going to Sydney and to her reunion with her relatives, Ruth, Elsa, and Lilly.

Vally passed away twenty-four years later in Sydney in 1987, a week before her ninetieth birthday. She passed away at home in her sleep, which was the best place and the best way to do it. Vally was blessed with a dedicated, wonderful daughter, Lisa. During her last years, she used to sit in her room, in her comfortable arm chair and, from time to time, utter the German word,"schrecklich" (terrible), probably whilst ruminating about her childhood, her first marriage to the Polish doctor and whatever other hardships she had to endure in life. When I think of her now, I hold no grudges. On the contrary, I respect her for her love and care for stray cats and dogs and for passing on her love of animals to Lisa. May she rest in peace.

Eventually, we were able to sell our nice, new home and repay our mortgage loan and debt under my contractual obligations to the company. We then purchased our BOAC airline tickets to Australia. We gave away the furniture and carpets to Chaim and his wife. Some of the furniture went to his relatives in Tel Aviv, who helped us with the transfer of our remaining money to Australia. Under Israeli law at that time, in 1962, we were not allowed to take money out of the country. So we gave our money to Chaim's relative in Tel Aviv, whereas their contact in Australia paid the equivalent amount in Australian currency to our contact in Sydney. This turned out to be just A£2,000—all that was left after our repayment of debt and mortgage.

On December 30, 1962, Chaim and his wife drove us—Lisa, one-year-old Iris, Vally, and me—to Lod Airport, where we boarded the BOAC plane, Australia bound.

————————

Six-plus years later, in 1969, Chaim wrote to me that the factory had been sold and that the new management had offered to pay for all our transfer costs if I was to agree to return to Israel and work in my old position as chief engineer. I respectfully declined their generous offer. By then, we had already purchased our home unit (condominium) in Bondi and were happily settled in Sydney, even though I still missed my friends and engineering work back in Israel.

One more interesting detail: In 1973, when I was general manager of Engineering & Research Pty. Ltd. in Sydney, my very good friend, Peter Cooke, the marketing general manager of our group of companies, visited Israel and naturally was keen to visit the factory where I worked. When he did so, the technical manager showed him the large, modern factory and also took him to what used to be my office in the Engineering Department. Peter insisted on sitting down in what used to be my chair at what used to be my desk in order to, in his words, "absorb the atmosphere." Peter was a very spiritual person! He was also very good at analysing people, so our managing director, to whom both of us were responsible, referred to him as the company psychologist.

In discussion with the technical manager, Peter was told that if it had not been for me, there would have been no gear production, and Israeli tanks would not have had the appropriate low-speed/high-power gearboxes to enable them to drive up the steep slopes of the Golan Heights in low gear and capture these heights from Syria during the Six-Day War in June 1967.

The design work that I did personally, as well as the design work done under my direction over the years—initiating gear production, first in the old factory and then in this modern plant; and training of the engineers and draftspeople in my team—were my main contributions to the Israeli industry.

Sadly, I did not get the opportunity to visit the factory again. I could have easily done so during one of my flights home, when returning from Europe to Sydney. However, visiting Israel without Lisa at my side would not have felt right, considering all our rich, shared memories there. Lisa had to stay home when I was overseas, looking after Iris and Vally.

Chapter 24

Destination Australia—The Third Long Journey

Iris was only one year and four months old when we left Israel. Our BOAC flight had stopovers in Karachi and Darwin. Long flights with babies are certainly not easy, but Iris was pretty good. An English lady who was also flying to Sydney predicted that before long, we would all adopt the broad Australian accent, but her prediction has not yet come true, even after fifty-one years in Oz. However, my Russian accent, I believe, was much more pronounced when I spoke Hebrew than when I speak English now.

I do not know how long these flights took in the sixties, including the two stopovers. By the time we arrived in Darwin on my thirty-second birthday, January 1, 1963, I had one of my splitting migraine headaches. This, unfortunately, was a frequent occurrence which stayed with me from the age of twenty-two at uni until about sixty-five, especially on weekends (after uni)—so-called *relaxation headaches.* Lisa and Vally survived the flight better than I did. The stopover in Darwin took longer than expected. We were tired and jet-lagged at the end of our flight but happy to finally arrive at Sydney's airport.

Our unaccompanied luggage arrived a couple of months later. It included two fairly large boxes of Russian engineering books, many of which were about different gear applications and designs, my first love in engineering. Sadly enough, I never again had the opportunity to use these books and be involved in gear design and manufacture. One of these books, a very large and rather thick English book with hundreds of pages, was entirely handwritten by Earle Buckingham and then printed, because he would not trust the printers to copy all his formulae and tables correctly. I can understand his concern and respect him for his conscientious work on this "gear design bible."

The first day or two in Sydney, we slept at the home of Lisa's relative, Ruth Widder. We then moved to a furnished holiday flat on Ramsgate Avenue, North Bondi, close to Ben Buckler Head, that Ruth had found for us. The famous Ben Buckler huge rock, weighing over two hundred tonnes, is believed to have been washed up from the bottom of the ocean during a huge storm in 1912. When we first saw it, the rock still had its two beautiful bronze mermaid statues sitting on it, created by the sculptor Luall Randolph and installed in 1960. One of these mermaids returned to the sea during another large storm in 1974 and has not been seen since. The second mermaid lost her tail and one of her arms during that same storm. It has since been removed by the local council for safekeeping. I always knew that mermaids do not live forever—but just fourteen years seems ridiculous!

Being a holiday flat that was available without long-term lease commitments, the Ramsgate Avenue unit's rent was quite high, so as soon as I found a job, we moved to a two-bedroom flat at 34/10 Ocean Street, Bondi. We furnished it with cheap furniture, some of which we bought at Norman Ross's auctions in Tempe, where the then-young Harvey Norman was their auctioneer. His raspy voice in his current TV commercials for the Harvey Norman Company has not changed since those auctions in 1963 (although he is now fifty-one years older). It is remarkable how little change, if any, occurs in our voices as decades fly by. Our vocal cords appear to be very stable.

The first or second evening in Bondi, Lisa and I went for a walk along the Bondi Beach Promenade and then had dinner at a Chinese restaurant. The promenade still had its ugly, rusty railings, which have since been exchanged for elegant, stainless-steel ones.

We knew Ruth well because she visited us in Tel Aviv together with her husband, Rafi, and their two young daughters, Judy and Jeanne. During Christmas, we all travelled to Beith Lechem (the House of Bread). Rafi was already very sick with MS but could still walk. In the years that followed, he gradually lost the use of all his limbs and his speech. He was bedridden and hospitalised for many years before passing away. Ruth and Rafi were Holocaust survivors.

It was Ruth who asked Lisa's other relatives, Paul and Mia Meyer, as well as Elsa and Lily Buckwell to provide us with sponsorships, a formality that was required for immigration to Australia. Years later we repaid this debt of friendship to Ruth when I negotiated on her behalf the purchase of her apartment, where she still lives today, at a price that she could afford. I also obtained for her a favourable mortgage from the Jewish Welfare Society, of which one of the Advance Industries directors was a committee member.

An Israeli car mechanic, Ben, a friend of Ruth's helped us choose a secondhand car at a Parramatta Road secondhand car dealer. It was a faded dark-red old model Holden, registration BKA 808, costing us A£800. This car was a good choice for the mechanic, because it provided him with ongoing repair work in the months that followed. Lisa and I took a few driving lessons around Bondi, in order to get used to driving on the left-hand side of the road. Whilst on that subject, let me add that Lisa and I both failed our first driving tests in Tel Aviv on the same steep, hilly street and for the same reason. How about that for solidarity?

A year or so later, after the repair costs of the secondhand Holden became too much to bear (and after we drove in it to the mountain resort of Katoomba and returned to Sydney in the rain without proper functioning windscreen wipers) the other relative of Lisa's, Paul Meyer, helped us to buy a standard, no-frills model new Holden, registration DAS 626, at a fleet discount, to which Paul was entitled as a taxi driver. That was the first new car we owned. Paul referred to the DAS registration as "drive Australia with Shell."

Paul also informed us about NRMA membership and car-insurance policies and recommended that we join the MBF private health insurance. We followed his advice and have been members with both organisations ever since for fifty-one years.

Chapter 25

BSP Industries Pty. Ltd.—
Difficult Adjustment

In January 1963, within two to three weeks after arriving in Sydney, I already found work as design engineer with BSP Industries Pty. Ltd. at Kippax Street, Surry Hills, for A£40 a week, which was considered a good salary in those days. The founder and owner of this company was the Austrian-born Fred Krebs. Tony Page from the UK, Bill Vrenegoor from Holland, and Paul Gross also from Austria soon became partners in the business. The main activity of this company at that stage was to engage and send out engineers and draftspersons to work as contractors on clients' premises.

Some projects were carried out on BSP's premises in Kippax Street. This was my prime engineering work, as long as it remained mechanical engineering and tooling design. I carried out a few successful projects and was promoted to chief engineer. This in-house design and drafting work kept on growing until it became necessary for BSP to rent additional, very much larger premises, close by in Foveaux Street. I was made manager of a newly formed separate BSP Consolidated Pty. Ltd. company for these in-house projects. The promotion meant a raise in salary and a brand-new, green Holden station wagon. This enabled us to sell our still rather-new Hoden sedan.

Both Tony and I interviewed new employees and contractors. Not surprisingly, our assessments of their engineering experience and personalities matched whenever both of us conducted an interview of the same applicant.

Eventually, we ended up with about 120 engineers and draftspersons, with half of them working on BSP's premises, for whom I was responsible. This growth was due to a tremendous diversification into different areas of engineering, including large projects in structural-steel and coal-washing plants—areas of engineering in which I had no experience whatsoever.

I found it difficult to adjust to the life in our new country. BSP's work gave me little satisfaction. I missed my friends in Israel and the production engineering in which I specialized and which I loved and enjoyed. To make things even worse, three years later, there was a downturn in the economy, which affected BSP's engineering business. The directors decided to retrench a large number of staff. This painful task was delegated to me. As Tony Page told me many years later, one of the other directors indulged in escapism—when faced with problems, he just went interstate.

I do not know how many people I had to retrench, but the most difficult retrenchment that I had to carry out was that of a young Russian draftswoman/tracer, who sat in my office crying and pleading with me not to retrench her.

Having finished my painful task, I reached an agreement with the remaining directors for me to leave BSP. We parted amicably, and I was allowed to keep on using my company car for another month or two. My assistant, an electrical engineer from the UK, Keith Higgins, and my loyal secretary from Austria, Renate, also left BSP.

Four-year-old Iris, playing in her toy corner in our flat at 34/10 Ocean Street, Bondi, used to call Renate on her toy telephone, saying: "Ring-e-ding, ring-e-ding, may I please speak to Tomate?"

I should also mention that, unbeknownst to me, a serious romance had developed between one of my five section leaders, Ron Martin, and my secretary, Renate. Ron and Renate got married soon after and are still happily married. I met with Ron several times at my consulting engineering business, but never with Renate. We've just exchanged Christmas cards for the last forty-seven years.

Shortly after my departure from BSP in 1966, I was contacted by the technical manager and the owner/founder of a company in Sydney, who heard of my departure from BSP. They were keen for me to join their company. The reason for this interest was a very successful design that I did for them shortly after I joined BSP.

They were building and exporting their own design of production machines all over the world, especially to the United States. One of their most important machines was beginning to struggle when competing in its production output on the international market. It was essential to try to increase the maximum speed at which the machine could perform reliably. Their engineers had tried everything, but above a certain speed, the large trays would spill the end product. During a visit by Tony Page to their office, looking for new design work, he was told by their owner/engineer that there was none at that time, but should we have spare design capacity, we would be welcome in trying to solve a difficult engineering problem as a challenge and fill-in job. The condition was that any payment by them for our services would be strictly limited to positive results, to be judged solely by them.

When Tony came back to the office and told me about the challenge, I undertook to examine the problem. This was a very large machine, I guess about five or six metres long and close to two metres wide, conveying trays filled with a certain product. It involved large levers located on either side of the machine that were supposed to turn over these trays without spilling the product in the trays at an increased speed. I soon realised that it was not the *speed* at which these trays were moved, but their *acceleration* that limited the machine's maximum production speed. I checked my assumption both graphically and analytically and came up with a simple design change in the existing lever system. Simple design solutions are always the best!

Now comes the drama. Our client had a brand-new machine in their loading dock, ready to be loaded on to a large semi-trailer and taken to the port for export to the United States. I presented my drawings and calculations to the owner, who was the designer of all their machines. He accepted that I had found the solution that eluded them for so long. To change the existing lever system, they had to oxy-cut the long levers on both sides of the machine and reweld them in a different angular position in relation to the driveshaft—no problem for their future machines, but this was a sparkling new machine, beautifully finished. There was no time to disassemble the machine for this modification. It had to be done whilst the machine remained fully assembled, without damaging any of the adjacent components. They did this successfully, tested and established the maximum speed, repainted the large levers, and shipped the machine overseas.

No doubt, many of these large machines were exported in the years that followed, costing, I assume, around $300,000 each at 2014's A$ value (or, say, the equivalent of three Jaguar cars, in case you are reading this in the years to come, by which time the A$ will have further devalued with inflation). No doubt, the company would have also upgraded all their many customers' existing machines that preceded this first new model and made their customers happy and more competitive. I met the technical manager at InterPack in Düsseldorf in 1969, the largest international packaging exhibition, where they exhibited their machines.

Forty-nine years have passed since that important design innovation. Many more machines must have been manufactured for the local market and primarily for export, providing ongoing employment for many local tradesmen. This gives me considerable personal satisfaction, especially when considering the unusual, dramatic circumstances of introducing this new design.

The company and this machine are both advertised on the Internet, but not surprisingly, the company founder and original owner/engineer and his technical manager are no longer listed amongst the contacts. However, judging by the surname, one of the owner's descendants is now the company's MD. This machine appears to be their main product.

Chapter 26

Advance Industries Ltd.—
Professional Reorientation

I decided not to join the machine-building company I described in the previous chapter. Instead, I applied for the position of chief engineer at Advance Containers Pty. Ltd. in Bankstown. In retrospect, I believe that was a wise (or rather lucky) decision, even though this required a complete change in direction in my engineering experience. No more production engineering, no more gears; I had to acquire knowledge and experience in plastic materials and plastics-processing technologies, of which I knew absolutely nothing. Once again, as our prime minister, Malcolm Fraser, used to say, "Life was not meant to be easy," and as I frequently add, "but it was not meant to be this bloody difficult either."

I probably should mention that before deciding to join the much smaller entrepreneurial company, Advance Containers Pty. Ltd., I did go for an interview to Borg Warner in Smithfield, a large company where all the gear boxes and rear axles for the Australian automotive industries were being produced. I was interviewed by the managers of several departments, each one of which was specialized in either design or production and of either transmission gear boxes or rear axles. Having gained a broader experience in a smaller manufacturing plant in Israel, catering for a smaller market, the thought of limiting myself to any of these four narrower specializations did not appeal to me. Besides, Smithfield was far away from Bondi, and we would have had to move closer to that factory.

When I joined Advance Containers in 1966, the company only produced a limited range of disposable plastic containers and tumblers from extruded polystyrene sheet. My first job at Advance Containers was to design a thermoforming press to be twice as big as and better designed than the presses that were being used at that stage at Advance. I engaged a contract-design draftsman from BSP, David Watson, and together we produced this larger press design and detail drawings. I then looked after its construction and successful commissioning. Within the next two years, I had another five identical presses built and another five sheet-extrusion lines commissioned. I also designed a wide range of disposable plastic containers and tumblers and the thermoforming tooling for their production.

In 1969, the managing director, Peter Ryba, sent me on a nine-week overseas trip to Tokyo, Milano, Varese, Zürich, Hägglingen, Näfels, Bern, Heilbronn, Düsseldorf, Köln, Bergneustadt, Copenhagen, Stockholm, Boston, Wilmington, Maryland State, Providence, New York, Newark, Washington, Toronto, Bolton, Saginaw, Beaverton, Chicago, Phoenix, San Francisco (twenty-seven destinations, with more than one company visited in some of them).

I visited many factories, took many photos with my little Minolta camera, and wrote long, detailed engineering reports on weekends, based on my ability to memorize all I saw and heard during my many office and factory visits. Needless to say, I would no longer be able to do so now, half a century later.

When I arrived in Milano from Tokyo via Rome, I felt jetlagged. I checked into the Hotel Cavalieri and went to a nearby large, crowded *ristoranti* with an open courtyard, where I was served a vegetable-and-meat salad with vinegar. Upon returning to the hotel, I got very sick, with dizziness, sweating, nausea, diarrhoea, and vomiting. I got frightened that, having come all the way to Europe, my business trip may end in complete failure, before it had hardly begun. In my desperation, I prayed to God for the first time in twenty-two years. (The last time I can remember praying was on my way to school before exams at the age of seventeen.) In my dizzy state, I virtually collapsed on my bed and fell asleep. When I woke up late that afternoon, I was healed and completely well, except for feeling very weak after what seems to have been food poisoning. Nevertheless, I managed to go for a walk to the Duomo di Milano and to the Castello Sforzesco, with its adjacent park.

This whole experience made a powerful impression on me. It was one of the first things I related to Lisa when I arrived home in Sydney.

My second stressful experience during that trip happened when I was visiting the head office and factory of a large packaging company in the United States. After a long day in the factory, collecting a lot of important information, I returned to my room at the Holiday Inn. I had to get ready to be picked up for dinner, to which I was invited by a senior executive and his wife. I did not think that I would be able to make it, because I was totally exhausted and perspiring profusely in the cold, air-conditioned hotel room. Anyhow, I did settle down, took a shower, and went out for dinner. My host happened to be Jewish. Whilst making conversation over dinner, my racist host posed the question, "Would you like us to export all our blacks to Australia?" I find racism in a Jewish person after the tragic events of the Holocaust experience especially cruel, stupid, and totally unacceptable.

The trip was a resounding success, and I was able to bring back to Advance extremely valuable information and introduce new technologies. However, my marathon nine weeks' tight itinerary, with so many objectives, was obviously way over the top. This was due to my inexperience, not realizing all the difficulties of such business travel and not allowing any time for relaxation.

As a result of my trip, we were able to introduce many new technologies at Advance. I introduced US Davies Standard polystyrene sheet extrusion, ordered German Illig thermoforming equipment, an Italian deep thermoforming press, Swiss Netstal injection-moulding machines, Swiss Polytype offset printing presses for containers and lids, large US plastic-recycling machines, and a large American Brown thermoforming machine. I was able to design a universal tool with interchangeable inserts to suit several sizes of our plastic cups. This made the Brown technology suitable to our smaller Australian market output requirements and thereby the first in Australia. In contrast to Australia, in the United States these types of machines, as well as much larger ones, can produce the same product on three shifts 365 days a year (except on leap years).

Since we were no competition to overseas and vice versa, I established an important exchange of information on new-product development with companies in Italy, Switzerland, Germany, Denmark, Sweden, and the United States.

With Peter Cooke's marketing strategies and my introduction of new packaging technologies and the design of a much-expanded new product range, Advance Packaging kept on growing and prospering. Advance was able to take over a custom injection-moulding company, Plastic Processors Pty. Ltd. in Alexandria. We imported several Swiss Netstal injection moulding machines for that company and further developed our packaging technology and increased our product range. Soon after that, Advance took over another two injection-moulding companies: Winton Plastics, a large company in Melbourne, and a smaller one in Adelaide, as well as a blow-moulding plant in Sydney.

In the meantime, Advance Ltd. had been listed on the stock exchange. I was appointed general manager of a newly formed subsidiary company, Advance Engineering & Research Pty. Ltd., responsible again directly to the managing director, Peter Ryba, giving me the centralized nationwide responsibilities for new factory and office-building construction, manufacturing equipment selection and procurement for all our plants nationwide, new-product development, patenting and overseas licensing negotiations. My dedicated and highly motivated engineering team consisted of twelve men, with two section leaders and my secretary, Ditas Ruiz (a mother of nine children, wife of a mentally ill husband, dedicated secretary and student of uni evening classes. How about that for motivation?)

I was able to have Advance Engineering & Research Pty. Ltd. recognized as an ARO—an approved research organization under the Commonwealth Industrial Research & Development Grants Act.

We had already built a large extension to our Bankstown plant, to more than double its size and absorb the Plastic Processors plant from Alexandria, including all the equipment for new technologies. The next step was the construction of a very large, modern plant in Clayton, Melbourne, to relocate Winton Plastics. I gave the responsibility for that project to one of my section leaders, Alan Taylor.

I travelled frequently overseas to Europe, the United States, and Japan, at least once a year, often on very short notice. These trips involved equipment inspection and purchases, attending trade exhibitions, licensing negotiations, e.g., with PCM in Ede, Holland; Bennett in Chicago; Cassalo in Hannover.

Cassalo was a particularly interesting case. One of the Advance directors had visited them but could not reach an acceptable licensing agreement. So Peter Ryba gave me the assignment. I flew off to Hannover and after two days of negotiations reached an agreement beyond everyone's expectations at Advance on royalties and other licensing terms for the exclusive rights to manufacture and market in Australia and New Zealand the stylish Cassalo plastic armchairs.

I then ordered what would become the largest in Australia 1,800-tonne injection-moulding press from Johns Hydraulics and the special tooling for moulding these glass-fibre-filled nylon Cassalo chairs from Krauss-Maffei in Germany.

Advance was a very healthy entrepreneurial company, privately owned by four directors. The managing director, Peter Ryba, to whom I was responsible, was and is a highly intelligent, capable person and experienced director with good technical knowledge and appreciation. He made it easy for us to progress, making quick capital-expenditure decisions with a minimum of red tape. I was indeed fortunate to have had the opportunity to work with and learn from a man like Peter.

After Advance Industries Ltd. had become a listed company on the stock exchange, several directors retired and sold their shares to a financial company that became the major shareholder. I believe that this company had no prior experience in our particular plastics-industry technologies and markets and were mainly interested in short-term financial profits. The only original shareholder and director left by then was Peter Ryba, and needless to say, he would have been outvoted at the board of directors' meetings. This whole situation must have somehow introduced tensions amongst senior management, of which I was one. Dedication and loyalty became a thing of the past, replaced by the selfish objectives of new, so-called professional managers. This, unfortunately, even affected the strong relationship between Peter Ryba and me.

Eventually, the new company direction and management style became unacceptable to me, and I resigned in November 1974, giving three months' notice. Peter Ryba tried in vain to find out from me what my plans were and where I was going. The fact is, I had no plans to go anywhere. We had long sessions at work and at his home. I left in January 1975, after an argument with the manufacturing manager and Peter Ryba, prior to the expiration of my three months' notice. Peter gave me a glowing letter of recommendation (see copy that follows), and four months after my departure, Peter released the company's share of my superannuation which, under the prevailing laws, he was not obliged to do because I was the one who resigned. I think he may have done so partly in response to a letter that I wrote to him on Yom Kippur, the Jewish Day of Atonement. We remained and still are good friends.

Asking my entire team to join me at my office and telling them of my decision in 1975 was just as hard as doing so in Israel in 1962. In the years to come, Alan Taylor, Peter Cooke, Tim Masuda, and I became equal partners in TC Handles Pty. Ltd., representing American, Swiss, and Italian plastics-processing equipment.

A year or so later, Peter Ryba left Advance Industries. Eventually, Advance Industries Ltd. was split up and sold, with Advance Packaging going to Hygienic Lilly and Advance Stationery going to Esselte. This was a rather sad end of what was once a progressive entrepreneurial company with an imaginative and dedicated board of directors.

Office party

Advance Engineering & Research Pty Ltd – 1974

140

Another office party !?

ADVANCE INDUSTRIES LIMITED

406 Marion Street, Bankstown, N.S.W. 2200 • Phone 708 2022 • Telex AA 24896 • Cables "ADIND" Sydney

March 10, 1975.

<u>TO WHOM IT MAY CONCERN</u>

I am writing this letter of reference with great reluctance for a friend whom I never expected to loose as a colleague before my own retirement, which is due in sixteen years.

Mr. Toren joined me as Development Manager of our packaging subsidiary in February 1966, and materially assisted in building up this relatively small company into the industry leader in the field of thermoformed plastic packaging.

In 1967 our Group formed an independent engineering and research subsidiary to look after all facets of development for the Group. Mr. Toren was appointed General Manager of this subsidiary, which became a registered research organisation under the terms of the Industrial Research & Development Grants Act.

Mr. Toren gradually increased his staff to number 16 engineers, draughtsmen and technicians and their work spanned building of premises for the Group, plant selection and procurement, process development, design of new products their tooling and trialling.

I consider Mr. Toren's engineering capabilities to be of a very high order and during his stay with the company he showed a degree of loyalty and dedication rarely exhibited in these times.

Mr. Toren regretfully left us after 9 years for reasons he has steadfastly insisted on keeping to himself, but which were not related to either his promotional ambitions, as he reported directly to myself, nor to his income, the level of which I believe he regarded as satisfactory.

I wish Mr. Toren every success in his future career and sincerely hope that he will find a niche which will challenge and interest him and enable him to enjoy the same happy working relationship we enjoyed for so many years.

P. RYBA, MANAGING DIRECTOR.

1-9 Edward Street, Oakleigh, VICTORIA. Telephone: 569 0901   24 Logan Street, Adelaide, SOUTH AUSTRALIA. Telephone: 51 3911
75 Weston Street, Brunswick, VICTORIA. Telephone: 38 9266   29 Finchley Street, Milton, QUEENSLAND. Telephone: 36 1300
9-11 Donovan Street, Osborne Park, WESTERN AUSTRALIA. Telephone: 24 1793

142

Chapter 27

Iris and Laura—The Next Two Generations

By the time I left Advance Industries in 1975, we were already living in our three-bedroom home at 316 Birrell Street, Bondi, which we purchased in 1967 with two mortgage loans. Our cash savings at the bank were only A$4,000, so the release of the company's contribution to my superannuation by Peter Ryba was very helpful. Iris was already in high school, having qualified for the prestigious, selective Sydney Girls High School.

Iris was a very good, diligent, and self-motivated student throughout primary and even more so throughout high school. She became Dux of Sydney Girls High School for 1979, as well as achieving the highest marks aggregate. Iris attributed her success in both of these considerable achievements just to good luck. I guess one would have to be extraordinarily lucky indeed to become first amongst five parallel classes of thirty girls, a total of one hundred fifty students—not just once, but twice in a row! Attributing her success to good luck makes even less sense, bearing in mind that Iris has an absolutely brilliant logical mind.

Studying medicine held no attraction for Iris because, being a vegetarian on conscientious grounds, she would not take part in any animal experiments. Law appeared boring and not creative enough. So Iris studied computer science at UNSW. She achieved very many high distinctions and distinctions but did not attend the graduation ceremony to receive her bachelor of science degree in computer science. She must have inherited my introverted attitude for such occasions.

Iris took time off early in her professional career to attend the esteemed Julian Ashton Art School full time, where she again distinguished herself. Iris is an extremely talented and accomplished artist. She creates the most beautiful paintings. All the walls of her and our home bear witness to it. Iris draws in pencil and ink and paints in watercolour, oil, and pastel, both from nature and still-life. Iris is extremely good with portraits. Unfortunately, it is hard to earn a decent living with honest art. Iris has had two exhibitions of her own.

Much of the so-called modern art that one sees now everywhere, including even at the Sydney Art Gallery is, in my opinion, an insult to one's intelligence. People who have no true feeling and appreciation for fine art admire it in the same way as the emperor's new clothes were admired in the Hans Christian Andersen story. Those so-called artists are, in my opinion, nothing more than good salespeople, with no heart for true art. The old Australian and overseas masters at our art galleries deserve more respect from us and should not have to share the gallery walls and space with those "pretend artists." Nor should we allow our tax money to be wasted on purchasing such nonsense pretend art, which within a century or two will end up in galleries' basements, never to be seen again by anyone, except art historians for analysis and critique, if that.

Iris has been working as a systems and business analysis consultant on a contractual basis for many years now, achieving success and recognition in her profession and a high income. Nevertheless, her heart will always be in fine art. Buying the correct lottery ticket would solve this problem.

From the time that Iris was born in 1961, her well-being and happiness became the most important objective in Lisa's and my life. This commitment was repeated thirty-two years later, when Iris' daughter, Laura, was born. We remained a close-knit family.

The year now is 2014, and Laura is twenty-one years old. After having successfully completed her HSC with an ATAR of 94.65 at the same prestigious, selective Sydney Girls High School as Iris had done, Laura has now completed her second year of her arts degree at Sydney Uni. I think her favourite subjects at uni so far have been art history and French. Laura has always been a very good drawer and has excellent, in-depth appreciation of art. Laura enjoys all her subjects and is happy with all her lecturers. Laura excels in English (always did, since primary school), as well as becoming fluent in French. Ever since early primary school, Laura amazed us and her teachers not only with her command of the English language but also with the remarkably imaginative content of her stories. It is Laura's intention to continue her Sydney Uni studies for a post-graduate MA degree.

Laura took up ballroom dancing a few years ago and now excels in Argentinean Tango Salon. Last year, Laura and Iris travelled to Buenos Aires. Iris is a very accomplished ballroom dancer, ever since before Laura was born. In recent years, she too concentrates on Argentinean Tango Salon. Recently, Laura and her friend Benjamin, who is also a very good dancer, took part in a Tango Salon competition in Sydney and won first prize! This entitles them to free return flights and free accommodation in Buenos Aires, which they are planning for later this year.

Most importantly, Laura has a beautiful, happy personality and a good heart. Like her mum and the rest of the Toren family, she loves animals and is a committed vegetarian. From birth, Laura has never tasted meat.

In chapter 6, I mentioned that not being able to play the piano and not speaking Mandarin turned out to be my first two serious regrets in life. The other two major regrets are that I failed to speak Russian to Iris, which I should have done from an early age and that I then repeated the same mistake with Laura. I could think of and make excuses, but that would not change anything. I believe that it is not only a loss of an important language but also a loss of a beautiful culture for Iris and Laura—losses for which I am to blame. It is also a serious loss for me personally because I have no one in my family with whom I can speak Russian. I sometimes also feel that this creates somewhat of a cultural divide between us. For instance, I cannot get Iris and Laura to listen and enjoy with me the beautiful Russian songs on my iTunes, with their wonderful, sentimental lyrics—sometimes typically Russian melancholic tunes and lyrics. I did, however, escort Laura to Bellevue Hill Russian School on Saturdays between the ages of six and eight, which would have given her some basic foundation that she may wish to build upon later in life.

I believe that the basic problem arises when there is only a single person in the family who speaks a certain language and tries to adhere to a certain culture. If there are at least two people, typically the mother and father, who speak that language and do so in the presence of the child, then the child learns to listen and communicate in that language from a very young age and picks up the correct pronunciation. The ability of children to adopt the precise pronunciation of their *clan,* right to the minutest nuance, is nothing short of a miracle. It fascinates me! This effortless ability of young children vanishes gradually by their early teens. The most difficult pronunciation and intonation of all languages undoubtedly is Mandarin. It definitely has to be acquired at a very young age.

To conclude, I do feel somewhat lonely, removed from my Russian culture. After my book is launched, it is my intention to reread some works by Dostoevsky, Tolstoy, Chekhov, Turgenev, and others, and if I have enough time left, I may even translate my life story into Russian, knowing that I would have a large audience waiting. Russians are curious to know what life is like outside their borders in the comparatively freer world. Let's face it—there is no truly *free* world.

Democracy also needs a facelift. Governments and oppositions should have the decency to agree, sacrificing a few tempting political point-scoring policies, and to allow the electorate to vote democratically from time to time for a predetermined number of national policies to become bipartisan: naturally, defence and security; everything relating to asylum-seekers' issues; climate-change policies; and possibly a few others that should be discussed and debated in parliament in a cooperative and civilised manner. Naturally, such reform would have to be debated at length, preferably under the guidance of retired federal judges and senior statesmen. This would have the tendency of restoring our confidence in politicians and positively involve the electorate in politics.

I believe that it is not for me to go into any details of Iris's personal life in my own life story. It is her choice, if and when she decides to do so. I asked Iris, and she agreed with that. Iris may wish to do so when she retires, when she will finally also be able to concentrate on her art. It seems to me that reflecting on one's life is best done later in life, with the benefit of additional experience and acquired wisdom, as well as more objectivity. I know that I could not have done it any earlier, nor would I have been inclined to do so.

———————

Good news! Last month, in April 2014, upon completion of her current IT contract, Iris has finally decided not to look for another contract, but instead to dedicate herself to art. Laura and I are completely supportive of Iris's decision.

Please see some of Iris's art on the pages that follow, as well as her website *http:// iristoren.com,* which includes portraits, landscapes and still life.

Pastel painting by Iris Toren
'Fontaine de l'Observatoire 1873
by Gabriel Davjoud'

Aquarel painting by Iris Toren 'Oriental Still Life with Tea Pot'

Iris Toren's drawing of daughter, Laura, in Gypsy Costume

Chapter 28

Germany, Singapore, Australia, United States—Perseverance

I spoke true when I said to Peter Ryba that I had no other position to go to. But nor was I going to look for one before first having a rest and giving serious consideration to some engineering ideas slowly germinating in my brain. After clearing the Advance cobwebs from my brain, I started thinking about designing and building a self-contained, 50-percent energy-saving and automatic material-recycling production line for various plastic products. Providing that these ideas could be materialised, the intention would be to sell this technology to an overseas company with exclusive international design, production, and marketing rights for the machine and its technology. Obviously, it was not an idea that I could have possibly realized at Advance. With all my other responsibilities, I would not have had the opportunity to concentrate on one major project, even less so during the turbulent final year. Regardless of the above-mentioned germinating engineering ideas and dreams, I would have resigned from Advance anyhow, because the writing was on the wall that with the new owners and the changed policies for Advance, I could no longer see a long-term future for myself. In fact, I was proved right by the resignation of Peter Ryba a year later, at which time I would have resigned anyhow.

I gave up the position of general manager of Advance Engineering & Research Pty. Ltd., a subsidiary of Advance Ltd., being responsible directly to the managing director, achieving the status of an approved research organisation, an ARO under the Commonwealth government's Industrial Research and Development Grants Act. I had been responsible for the company's R&D, new-product development and patenting, licensing negotiations, equipment procurement for the Australia-wide group of Advance companies, and special-purpose machine design. I gave up a private secretary and a large private office, as well as a great team of loyal people with whom I shared mutual respect and who did not want me to leave. I had a good salary, a company Diners Club card, and a luxury Statesman company car. The managing director was trying hard to talk me out of leaving. Making the decision somewhat more difficult was the fact that Lisa and I had only savings of A$4,000 in the bank. There was a certain déjà vu with the resignation from my position in Israel, except that the financial sacrifice in Israel was much greater.

Even though I believed there may have been two serious prospects overseas for the new technology, I also knew that it would certainly not be easy to reach an agreement with these companies. Nevertheless, I was determined to take a risk, for the chance of succeeding with my engineering dream for either licensing this new technology or selling it outright.

I cannot mention any details here of this new technology, the products for which it can be used, and the names of companies and people with whom I did eventually negotiate, because these companies may have commercial reasons for wishing to keep this confidential.

Germany

My first attempt was with the general manager of a large, modern plastics-processing company in Germany, whom I had visited in the past. I believed that he would be interested in such a new technology concept. After having left Advance, I wrote to him, and sure enough, he invited me to come to Germany at his company's expense, to submit an offer to him for the supply of the design and related know-how. I accepted his offer, flew to Germany, and on the following day proceeded to his factory. I was invited to lunch, together with several other overseas visitors.

He enjoyed showing off his modern plant to overseas visitors and "holding court" over lunch. We were all introduced to each other with accompanying introductory comments by our host. When my background was mentioned briefly, as far as he knew it, he made the inappropriate observation, *"Na ja, wir hatten doch einen Führer!"* (Well, we did have a Führer!), and it seemed to me that in doing so, he appeared to dismiss the guilt of the rest of the German nation. (After all, it is a known fact that nobody in Germany knew anything about the concentration camps that were run somewhere far away by the Martians, and the murder of 6 million Jews, 24 million Russians with more than half of them civilians, 2.5 million gentile Poles, etc., which appears to be just ongoing malicious propaganda.)

The price that I asked for the development and supply of my technology was more than he had envisaged, but I stood my ground and was not prepared to bargain. He handed me a cheque for my services and disbursements and said that it was good in any case that I came because it gave me another opportunity to visit my mother in Hiddessen. So, regardless of what appeared to be a simplistic historical analysis, and taking into consideration the possibility of my wrong interpretation of it, we parted as friends.

Singapore

The new technology had the big advantages of energy-saving, automatic material recycling, especially for remote areas of developing countries, as well as the production flexibility of these self-contained production lines.

All these technical and cost advantages were not lost on the Singaporean company director, a very astute businessman and experienced manufacturer. He was also on the board of directors of the Singapore Group of Companies. He was a lovely fellow, and we became good friends. Peter Cooke and I spent many happy Chinese dinners for the next few months discussing with him the possibility of introducing the technology into Southeast Asia, with him frequently saying in his soft voice and with a gentle smile on his face, "What to do, what to do?" He successfully did do his part in these negotiations!

The board of directors accepted our offer to supply them with the technology and know-how for a lump-sum down-payment plus equity in the new company that would be established for the promotion of this technology and equipment throughout Southeast Asia. Equity was a generous bonus offered by them before we even suggested it.

They recognized the particular suitability of these self-contained machines for many remote locations of Southeast Asia. In fact, it was the only practical and feasible option for local decentralized manufacture.

Unfortunately, there was a catch, in spite of their attractive offer and the interesting longer-term equity prospects. Their prerequisite was for me to move to Singapore, so that the equipment design and manufacture could take place there. This was a reasonable request on their part but unacceptable to us, primarily because Iris was still attending high school. The hard-to-bear hot climate (and the forest-burning air pollution of future years) were not known to us at that stage. Therefore, in retrospect, our choice of staying in Oz was definitely the right one, bearing in mind not only Iris's education but also Lisa's asthma. However, I must say that it would have been absolutely lovely to see and hear Iris speak Mandarin, which she undoubtedly would have been doing now.

Australia

With both the German and Singaporean prospects having been eliminated, the next opportunity was with an Australian company. The MD was very keen to acquire the technology, but internal company problems seemed to prevent him from doing so. So, after lengthy deliberations involving my friend Peter Cooke, he decided against it.

Next target—the United States!

Chapter 29

The Big Breakthrough—Success at Last!

Germany, Singapore, Australia—Three Down, One to Go!

The American company was next on the list. Contact was made, once again through Peter Cooke. Many meetings with the local GM followed. Finally, it was decided that I should accompany him on a trip to Europe to inspect available technologies and similar products we would be producing with the proposed technology. This exploratory trip covered Milano, Lyon, Paris, and Zürich. I cannot remember if Köln or Stockholm were also included. My good Swiss friend, Cuno Hunkeler, was very helpful, as usual, by collecting for us invaluable samples from different European companies. We needed these samples to complete our product-range assessment.

Upon my return to Australia, the GM submitted a feasibility study report to the MD at the head office, supporting the proposal to go ahead with this technology. Next came the negotiations with the two American executives who came to Sydney for this purpose. Our conference took place at Sebel House at King's Cross. In typical American fashion, their advice was, "Bring your lawyers with you." I did not follow their advice. With my licensing-negotiations experience, I preferred to keep the lawyers out at that stage. Lawyers tend to complicate matters at an early stage of negotiations and can even jeopardize them. We reached an in-principle agreement without lawyers.

Next followed the drafting of a complex legal agreement, which took several weeks to complete and was brilliantly executed by my good friend, Frank Liddy, the senior partner of Taylor & Scott Solicitors of Elizabeth Street, Sydney. Frank used to say to me, "Why don't you come to my home on Saturday morning and we shall chew the rag?" Chew the rag we did, weekend after weekend. Based on Frank's creative and imaginative analysis of the comprehensive sale of this innovative technology, we ended up with two perfect complementary legal documents, the second of which consisted of an agreement to sell the exclusive international rights for the machine design, the exclusive international manufacturing rights, know-how and expertise, and a commitment by me to never again engage in this technology and industry. Frank used to say that this was like "selling your corner store and committing yourself never to open another one." Brilliant analogy! This eventually resulted in a financial advantage in relation to the lump-sum settlement. I honoured my commitment and never worked again in that industry. Thank you, Frank. We remained good friends.

A few years later, His Honour Francis Liddy was appointed to the bench of the Industrial Court. Peter Cooke and I visited him at his home for family celebrations, and for lunch at his very impressive chambers, diagonally opposite the Intercontinental Hotel in Sydney.

Chapter 30

The New Technology—My Most Important Project

This was a multimillion-dollar project, for which I was committing myself to design a complex machine for mass production of plastic products, with innovative automatic features that had never been attempted before in these types of machines for the production of similar products. The design also had to include all the necessary auxiliary equipment to create a complete automatic production line. After completion of the design within one year, all of this equipment had to be constructed under my supervision within a certain timeframe and within a specified budget, which meant that it also involved a substantial financial risk for me. After the machine had been constructed, delivered to the specified location, and installed together with all the auxiliary equipment, and after all the detailed engineering drawings and specifications for this specific technology had also been delivered, I would have to commission the equipment and demonstrate the production of an agreed, specified product of good commercial quality at an agreed production rate. I also had to hand over a complete set of engineering assembly, subassembly, and detail drawings and specifications.

My first priority was to engage two of my proven coworkers: David, a first-class machine-design draftsman, and Natasha, a first-class draftsperson, both of whom had worked with me before and were keen to join me in this project. I rented an office in Crows Nest, which was located halfway between David's and my homes and very close to Natasha's home.

I then produced a time schedule and costing for the design and construction of each of the machine's subassemblies. My friend and solicitor, Frank Liddy, assisted me with some other important business matters related to this project. As you can see, the business relationship with Frank developed into a true friendship. A couple of years later, after Frank was appointed to the bench of the industrial court, I enjoyed having lunch with him on several occasions in his very impressive judge's chambers.

Back to the description of our design task: needless to say, there was no time for designing and testing any prototype machine or even any of its subassemblies. All aspects of various functions in the design had to be thought through and visualised with the utmost of care, and all the subassembly and detail drawings had to be prepared with no room for any dimensional errors.

Programmable logic controls (PLCs), e.g., by Omron, were not yet commercially available in those days. We prepared charts of the complex sequential controls, with interlocks where required, to actuate the micro-switches and proximity switches required for the proper cycling of the reciprocating machine and the specific process control. Our charts were then translated by a contract electronics engineer for the manufacture of a custom-made electronic control cabinet.

Some of the automated functions that were incorporated in our design had never even been attempted before by European companies that manufactured these types of plastic products.

To make a long story short, we completed the design and construction of the machine on time and within the allocated budget. David did an excellent design job, and Natasha performed with her usual accuracy and speed, all under my supervision and guidance. I then obtained competitive quotations for construction of these subassemblies, placed orders, and supervised the final stages of construction of all the subassemblies with different toolmaker companies. We then assembled all these subassemblies into the complete machine. We could only dry-cycle the machine in Sydney—cycle it without plastic material. I hired a truck, and the machine was loaded onto it at the workshop where we did all the final assembly work. The machine was the only load on the truck, and it was driven directly to the specified location interstate, without being reloaded at a depot, which is the normal procedure for interstate transport.

When the day came to test the performance of the machine with plastic, the American hierarchy, who happened to be in Australia, came down to the factory floor before we had a chance to test the machine ourselves and make the necessary adjustments. When we started the machine, it closed and did not return to its open position. The American executives, who had no idea what they were looking at, turned around and left. Because the machine was now operating with plastic, compared to Sydney, where we were only dry-cycling it, we had to compensate for the presence of plastic by reducing the stroke of the machine. This adjustment took less than one minute for us to do; however, the uninvited guests who witnessed our "failure" had already gone.

After the rest of the production line was installed, everything worked perfectly. We achieved the nominated production output and the required product quality, with the product automatically and neatly stacked in the multiple parallel chutes, ready to be dropped into shipping cartons.

Having passed this crucial commissioning test with flying colours, and after handing over two complete sets of reproducible drawing prints and operating manuals to the American company, my contractual obligation was fulfilled to their complete satisfaction. I received a cheque for half the lump-sum payment, and six months later received the second half, all as per our agreement.

Our client immediately ordered a second production line. It was built identical to the first one (without requiring a single modification in our detail drawings and specifications). Our client also asked us to design the special tooling for another three products. We carried out this additional work on an hourly rate payment basis. To expedite this work, I engaged another one of my ex-Advance design draftsmen.

This was the successful end of this important project.

Chapter 31

Financial Security—And Peace of Mind

As you recall from an earlier chapter, I took the risk of resigning from a well-paid position of general manager of the centralized engineering subsidiary of the Advance Industries Ltd. nationwide group of companies. Resigning was not an easy decision, but I had to take it to fulfil my dream of designing an innovative plastics-processing machine and becoming financially independent and establishing my own consulting engineering firm. There was no guarantee that my design concept of this machine would work. Therefore, entering into a contractual commitment with the American company required considerable confidence and determination.

Having received the first half of the lump-sum payment from the American company upon the successful completion of this project, I made an unexpected bonus payment to David for his good work. Then, after receiving the second half of the payment, Lisa and I promptly drove to my friend and silent partner, Peter Cooke, to deliver a cheque for his share of the lump-sum payment received. We gave him 50 percent of the total lump sum, which was very generous, considering his limited occasional involvement in this project. Peter was a very experienced marketing professional but was unable to assist with the conceptual process and machine design or the construction of the equipment. However, his initial involvement was an important contributing factor in the eventual success.

Lisa and I decided to invest our money in income-producing residential real estate, so that the money should remain "safe as houses." We bought two three-bedroom and two two-bedroom condominiums. All the properties that we purchased in 1977 and 1978 were located in the Bondi Heights and Bondi Junction areas, firstly because we intended to manage them ourselves and secondly because we could foresee their capital appreciation with the future Eastern Suburbs railway link, the future Bondi Junction Mall, Shopping Centre, and Sid Einfeld Bypass developments, all of which *did* eventually happen. We bought all four properties for cash, without any mortgages. Had we applied at least modest mortgages to these four properties, paying them off with the rental income received, we could have stretched our cash to buy another one or two properties. This would have been the way to maximise our investment in the long term. We were aware of this, but to Lisa and me, peace of mind without mortgage debts was more important than maximising our investments. To achieve this peace of mind through financial security was important to both of us because we experienced difficult times in our earlier lives. This is also why we would not risk our hard-earned money on the share market. We believed, and I still do, that dealing with shares should be left to those who have some solid knowledge of the stock market, rather than rely on lucky guesses.

All four units were, naturally, chosen by Lisa, who had an uncanny talent for finding and evaluating real estate. Lisa could recognize buildings in the eastern suburbs from photos and know exactly where they were located. Lisa could easily identify all the major buildings in the city when looking at the distant skyline from our Bondi Junction balcony. She could quickly walk through a unit or house and accurately assess all its positive and negative features. Lisa's favourite activity was helping our friends to find new homes. As I am writing this, I have just counted six of Lisa's success stories in helping her friends.

At the end of each tenancy, we always fixed up these condominiums without any compromises on quality of renovation. I used to say, "Nothing is ever too good for Lisa's tenants!" Besides, it helped us to attract better new tenants and possibly receive higher rents. We were very responsive to our tenants' special requests, and we have accumulated a whole stack of letters from grateful tenants, which were written after they moved on. I must admit that a contributing factor to their satisfaction was our reluctance to increase rents for good tenants. I think it is called reciprocity.

If you estimate the value of these four properties in today's dollar values and include my friend's share, you will get an idea of the amount of money I received for the new technology I developed, equivalent to the value of eight new home units in high-rise buildings. Had I given you the actual amounts in dollars negotiated in 1976, it would not have meant anything to you today.

In 1979, I established my consulting engineering firm, Lesete Pty. Ltd. After earning some more money, we bought a small one-and-a-half-room unit in Randwick, once again with no mortgage. Some of these properties are in the name of our Hacima Pty. Ltd. company, and others were in Lisa Toren's name, in order to minimise land tax. We did not adopt an extravagant lifestyle, because we wanted to leave all these properties to Iris and Laura for their financial security. I hope the time will come when Iris and Laura will be able to fully appreciate this, even without having to experience any financial hardships in life, as Lisa and I did, to fully gain such appreciation. My hope has always been that, after my demise, when Iris inherits all these properties, she will be able to retire from her systems/business analysis profession and dedicate herself to her fine art and painting, which she loves and in which she excels. I am confident that this will give her satisfaction, happiness, and the recognition of being the outstanding artist that she is.

Even though, generally speaking, our family kept a modest lifestyle, we did travel regularly to Hawaii together with Iris, and later on with Iris and Laura. We stayed at the Royal Hawaiian Hotel, known as the Pink Palace. This was Lisa's and my "happy place." Lisa fell in love with Hawaii after reading James Michener's novel, *Hawaii*. Our first trip to Hawaii took place in 1988 after I sold the name and goodwill of my consulting engineering firm. Needless to say, our Hawaiian destination was Lisa's choice and initiative. The Royal Hawaiian was her and my choice. Over the years, we made many friends amongst the staff of the RH Hotel.

Lisa's and my other extravagance during our last ten years together was going out for vegetarian buffet every Saturday evening and every Sunday morning at the Shangri-La Hotel in the city. We became good friends with many members of the restaurant staff, some of whom visited us at home with their partners. Amongst them were recent arrivals from China, Thailand, and Korea. We were able to help some of them with the preparation of professional-looking résumés.

Our whole family also travelled to Europe several times—to Vienna, Salzburg, and its surrounding townships and lakes, to Zurich, Luzern, St. Moritz, Paris, London, Tokyo, and Kyoto.

After Lisa fell ill, Iris and Laura travelled on their own to Rome, Venice, Paris, London, Los Angeles, and New York, where they visited many museums and art galleries and took many photos of famous sculptures, which enabled Iris to create some magnificent paintings. Please see her pastel painting of the nineteenth-century Fontaine de l'Observatoire statue by Gabriel Davioud in Paris at the end of chapter 27.

Chapter 32

Lesete Pty. Ltd—Consulting Engineers

In 1979, I was contacted by the GM of a company in Melbourne, offering me a long-term engineering-design project. He knew me from another large project that I'd done for him in the past.

I formed the company Lesete Pty. Ltd. Consulting Engineers and rented an office in Challis House at 10 Martin Place, Sydney. I engaged David, who worked for me at Advance and also during the large American project. David and I ended up working together for twenty-two years altogether (another lucky twenty-two).

We designed and looked after the manufacture of several special-purpose machines for the manufacture of large, high-density hmwHDPE bags with glued-on PP strapping, as well as designing and patenting special PP buckles for the strapping of these bags after they were loaded with the product for which they were intended. One of these special-purpose machines for the hot-melt gluing of the PP strapping to these bags was fully automated with Omron PLC (programmable logic controls).

In 1981 and 1982, David and I travelled to Dai Nippon in Tokyo on behalf of our client, regarding aseptic long-life packaging equipment for the packaging of milk as well as acidic fruit juices in bag-in-box packs. Two years later, Peter Cooke and I also accompanied a director of that company to Düsseldorf to assist with the negotiations for the Australian representation of another long-life pack. I served both as engineer and German/English interpreter. We also designed and patented a special tap for the Australian bag-in-box wine cask and a milk-dispenser tap, including the design of a mini-fridge for milk.

We were also engaged by the Spastic Society of Victoria to design a case for a communication aid for speech-impaired people.

Marblo Holdings Pty. Ltd.

In 1985, I was approached by Dr. Karim Obaidi—the inventor of a special blend of plastic material, known commercially as Marblo, for kitchen bench tops, airport check-in counters, wall cladding, and many other applications—to design an extremely large horizontal press for the casting of multiple large panels. This press ended up being about six metres long and over two metres wide. The first press was manufactured and put into production in Sydney. A second press was exported to China as part of a complete turnkey manufacturing licence agreement with a Chinese government state-owned enterprise. Marblo Holdings was the first Australian company to do so. I feel very proud that such a large machine we designed was exported to China.

Dr. Karim Obaidi is a qualified civil engineer and a remarkable man who was not only able to develop the special formulations for a very extensive range of Marblo plastic materials but also had the tenacity and amazing perseverance to build his company up from grassroots. He told me about some of the details of his struggle in achieving this objective. I am proud that I was able to assist him in that struggle in a small way. You can obtain additional interesting information about Marblo from the Internet.

We did one more very large project at Lesete Pty. Ltd. Consulting Engineers for an Australian government authority. This was our last project. It took eight of us, myself included, two and a half years to complete. I had to rent a second, much larger office in Challis House for this project. Client confidentiality prevents me from revealing any information and details about this project. After successfully completing this project in 1988 and handing all the engineering drawings to our client, I sold the name *Lesete* and the goodwill of the company, and limited my engineering activity to my home office under the name Toren Consulting Pty. Ltd.

Chapter 33

TorenPak CR/SF Pharmaceutical Packaging Innovation

After the sale of the name and goodwill of my engineering consulting company, Lesete Pty. Ltd., I concentrated on the design and patenting of child-resistant (CR) and senior-friendly (SF) pharmaceutical packaging for tablets, both in bottle-dispensing form (dispensing one tablet at a time) and as folding blister packs.

My patented, innovative, user-friendly CR/SF blister pack for tablets and capsules was 'Highly Commended' in the 'Packaging Innovation Award' category and a 'Shortlisted Finalist' in the 'Consumer Responsiveness Award' category at the International Packaging Industry Awards in London.

Professional articles were published by the following United States and UK pharmaceutical and packaging magazines:

Packaging Innovations
Packaging News
Pharmaceutical Marketing
Packaging Week
Packaging magazine
Pharmaceutical Technology
Packexpo.com
Ben Miyares' Packaging Management Update

When a single conventional blister pack is removed from its outer carton and kept in a lady's handbag, the foil is susceptible to being punctured through contact with hard objects (e.g. keys, coins, and lipstick), causing the exposure of tablets to contamination, oxidation, and humidity, as well as becoming more accessible to children. My user-friendly Folding Blister Pack solved this problem by enabling the blister card to be folded in half and locked, with only the tough plastic film on the outside and none of the brittle aluminium foil left exposed to accidental damage.

In spite of the pack winning prizes at the prestigious International Packaging Industry Awards in London and the positive evaluations in all the professional pharmaceutical packaging press in the United States, UK, and Australia, I was not able to license the manufacturing rights to any of the head offices of the multinational pharmaceutical companies in Switzerland, UK, and New Jersey, basically because, I believe, they had no financial incentive to change from their existing packs that were successfully selling in the international markets. Although the manufacturing costs were almost identical, the blister-packaging machines would have to be retooled.

Nevertheless, in 1993, I got very close to finalising a licensing agreement with a large pharmaceutical company in the UK, after producing a customised design for one of their products, including prototype tooling and samples. We signed a twelve-month first-option agreement, for which I received a substantial lump-sum payment. The person I concluded these negotiations with said to me that this pack was *"too good not to be used."* Unfortunately, he was transferred to another division of this large company, and without him, our project died.

Another interesting example, typical of the pharmaceutical industry's frequent takeovers, was when I was asked to produce a customised blister-pack design for a Swiss company. After satisfying their requirements with a very functional and attractive design, and whilst discussing the terms of the manufacturing licensing agreement, the company was taken over by another Swiss pharmaceutical company.

The person I was negotiating with at the *first* company joined the *second* company and recommended to their product development manager to engage me for the design of a folding blister pack for one of their tablets. Unfortunately, after this design was completed, but before the negotiations could be finalised, this *second* company was taken over by a *third* Swiss pharmaceutical company. Amazing!

In 2000, I travelled to Zurich and, together with my representative for the UK and Europe, Mr. Colin Scaife, met the senior project leader for packaging and device development of this *third* company. We discussed both the *child-resistant single-tablet-dispensing bottle* and the *folding blister pack*. We left samples for him of both packs, and later I sent him several layouts of folding blister packs. He informed us that our innovative packs were placed on their shortlist for imminent consideration. Unfortunately, a couple of months later, he moved to another company, and the contact was lost.

Three companies in fast succession of prospective licensees. A very dynamic industry indeed!

Other negotiations with American companies followed after the appointment of pharmaceutical-industry consultants, Montesino Associates LLC of DE, United States as our international representatives of TorenPak™ CR/SF Folding & Locking Blister Packs and TorenPak™ CR/SF Tablet Dispensing Bottles.

Chapter 34

Lisa—My Beloved Wife and Life's True Friend

We should all count our blessings. Unless we fully appreciate God's blessings, they are wasted on us. Certainly, my extraordinary blessing in life has been having Lisa as my wife and my life's precious true friend. We were happily married for fifty-four years. On November 6, 2009, after a long and difficult illness, my beloved Lisa passed away. During my difficult grieving time, I keep reminding myself of the fact that I must be grateful for the blessing that I received, and most importantly, for the fact that Lisa suffers no more. I also tell myself that because I was so blessed with such an extraordinary wonderful partner in life, I must now also be prepared to accept the depth of her loss.

Lisa suffered from gradually worsening allergic asthma for the last twenty-four years of her life. Nine years before her passing, Lisa lost her hearing in both ears within just two weeks, instead of being able to adjust to a gradual loss of hearing over a period of several years. She chose to have a cochlear implant. However, this did not enable her to listen to music, radio, TV, or to communicate on the phone. We can only try to imagine how it would feel to suddenly lose one's hearing and, after a difficult operation and the adjustment that followed, to be able to partially hear metallic-sounding speech, whilst attempting to lip-read the rest, as Lisa did. In spite of all these burdens, Lisa maintained her usual cheerful, friendly nature and, in her selfless way, was more concerned with her family's minor ailments than with her own serious health problems.

Last year, Lisa was hospitalized several times and was eventually diagnosed with heart failure, secondary to amyloidosis, which brought with it myeloma, requiring chemotherapy. After three months of chemotherapy, Lisa decided to discontinue the

THOMAS TOREN

treatment, so as not to intensify and prolong her suffering. Lisa's breathlessness and weakness were caused by the combination of heart failure, water retention, and asthma, with just 26 percent lung capacity and less, as the end was approaching.

Three weeks before her death, whilst being cared for by Iris and me at home, Lisa called me one morning to say, *"Tommy, the time has come for me to go back to hospital. We had a good long life together, and I reached the ripe old age of seventy-six. We all have to die sooner or later."* At the same time, in order to speed up the process and stop her suffering, Lisa made the courageous decision to stop all her medication, except for her asthma puffers and to reduce eating and drinking to an absolute minimum. After two weeks, Lisa could only slowly move her head and arms, and during the third week, Lisa could neither hear nor speak. Nevertheless, one day before her passing, she still smiled for a close friend, Dr. Ellen Campion, who visited her, and threw thank-you kisses to nurses who assisted her. This was the kind of person Lisa was—kind, gentle, generous, selfless, and extremely brave and decisive when making and carrying out important, difficult life decisions. I only remember Lisa crying briefly once throughout this long, agonizing ordeal. No doubt, selfless to the end, she was controlling herself in our presence because she wanted to reduce our pain of watching her agony.

During Lisa's twenty-two days in Wolper Hospital, Iris slept in a makeshift bed next to her every night, whilst I spent all day with her and took her for walks in her wheelchair along the leafy streets surrounding the hospital. We were at Lisa's bedside when she drew her last breath in the evening of November 6, 2009.

For the last four months of her life, Lisa had been asking her palliative-care doctors to expedite her death when the end was near. Because of Lisa's breathlessness and weakness, she lived in constant fear of suffocation—and suffocate she did, whilst the nurses were hastily preparing to try to pump out the accumulated liquid from her lungs. The memory of Lisa's last attempted breath will haunt me for as long as I live.

Lisa's torture could and should have been avoided. Our politicians should have taken the time in recent years to discuss the issue of euthanasia in a practical, humane, and compassionate way, knowing that many terminally sick people are pleading for their suffering to end. Our politicians could have appointed a panel of medical and legal experts to come up with practical solutions to allow euthanasia, whilst protecting the patients from themselves and from unscrupulous relatives or carers to prevent any abuse of the law. This has been successfully achieved in Holland and Switzerland. Unfortunately, it seems that our politicians are still afraid of the influential leaders of all religions and denominations. This will result in more suffering of terminally sick people who will be denied euthanasia. Eventually, our rapidly aging population, the shortage of hospital beds, and the increase in hospitalization costs will force this issue to be finally addressed and resolved.

We considered the possibility of travelling to a clinic in Switzerland that offers help through euthanasia, but at that stage, Lisa was already too weak to travel, even with the assistance of a nurse. We also considered and investigated the possibility of doing it ourselves at home, using helium gas, but I could not bring myself to do so, especially when considering the risks involved as a result of my inexperience, which could have left Lisa paralysed instead of relieved from her suffering. The instructions in two books that Iris bought on euthanasia urged people to reduce such risks by conducting several rehearsals of this act. I do not think that Lisa was ready for such rehearsals three weeks before her passing. Instead, Lisa asked me to take her to hospital, still counting on her palliative care doctor that he "would not let her suffer."

———————

Following is the eulogy that I delivered at Lisa's funeral:

Lisa, Iris, Laura, and I thank you for coming.
I mention Lisa's name, because I believe that Lisa is here with us in spirit.

Lisa was born in 1933 in Holland, daughter of (Yentel) Valesca Fischer and (Avraham) Darlee Dju.

In 1939, the family fled from Nazi-occupied Danzig to Shanghai, and after the war, in 1946, returned to Vienna, the birthplace of Lisa's mother.

In 1948, when the State of Israel was proclaimed, Lisa and her mother migrated to Israel and settled in the coastal town of Nathanya.

Lisa and I met in 1952 in the army, soon after Lisa's conscription and a fortnight before my discharge. We met at the army camp cinema, where I approached her, saying that I recognized her after seeing her once in Nathanya.

She asked me for a book she could read, and I brought her Orwell's *1984*.
The year 1984 seemed a long way in the future.
Now it is in the far-distant past.

One year later, in 1953, we met again on the beach of Nathanya.
We were married in 1955 in Haifa, where I was studying.
There were three people present at the wedding (two people under the *chupa* plus one other) on the roof of the Rabbanut near Herzl Street.
We have been happily married for fifty-four years.

In 1961, our daughter, Iris, was born in Tel Aviv, and the following year, when she was just one year and four months old, we came to Australia.

Lisa has been the most wonderful, kind, loving, generous, and unselfish wife to me, to her mother, to Iris and to Laura.

Lisa was always completely supportive of Iris's hopes and aspirations and gave Iris so much loving help in the care and upbringing of Lisa's adored granddaughter, Laura.

Lisa's gentle kindness and compassion was shown also in her love of all animals, and she was a vegetarian for the last thirty-four years.

Lisa was an extraordinarily courageous person, which was shown in the way she accepted her illness and death, and in having to face her deepest fear of not being able to breathe. Four weeks ago, when any prospects of recovery were no longer possible, and because euthanasia is not available, Lisa decided to stop her medication, and to reduce the intake of food and liquid to an absolute minimum, in order to expedite the process of her demise, saying that we had a good life together, that she reached the age of seventy-six, and everybody has to go sooner or later. She never complained or cried, which I believe is because she did not want to distress us.

Being the unselfish person that she was, right up until the end, she was more concerned with her family's relatively minor ailments, rather than her own severe illness.

Good-bye, dear Lisa; thank you for being my wife and my life's best friend.
I shall always keep loving you.

Until we meet again, Lisa, we will not be able to share any details of our fifty-four years' beautiful, rich memories.

We love you, and shall miss you terribly.
It will take time before I will be able to imagine a world without you.

Shalom v'lehitraot [Peace, and until we meet again]

The service was conducted at the Temple Emanuel synagogue, which is the liberal synagogue that Lisa attended regularly for the last ten years or so. Lisa attended the synagogue on weekdays, when there were virtually no people present. I reproach myself now for not having accompanied Lisa at least sometimes during her prayers there. I also reproach myself for spending too much time working—precious time that I could and should have spent with Lisa. Please forgive me, Lisa.

I think of Ray Charles's beautiful song, "I Can't Stop Loving You," which reflects my feeling when he sings, "They say that time heals a broken heart, but time has stood still since we've been apart." I know that this pain can never be healed.

Next week will be the fourth anniversary of Lisa's passing.

Amongst the many Russian songs, the two that express my feelings best are: *"Мне не забыть тебя - я знаю!"* ("Never Can I Forget You—I Know") and *"Глаза твои"* ("Your Eyes").

The feeling that sometimes suddenly comes over me is the realization that Lisa's presence—yes, her live presence—is gone forever, and just for a second or two, this seems *strangely unreal* to me. What I mean is that Lisa will never again suddenly appear at the entrance to my study, and I will never again be able to see her sitting in her armchair when I enter the lounge room. I will not hear her voice and see her smiling face—I repeat, her presence is gone irrevocably forever. All these thoughts race through my mind for a couple of seconds when this strange feeling suddenly hits me; I break down and cry just for a minute or two—and then I feel calm, empty, and very sad.

When I pray now, I always ask God to make sure that Lisa does not feel lonely without the children and me and that Lisa and I should try not to look back but instead, we should both look forward to our next happy meeting and life, when we shall stay together for eternity. When that time comes and we first see each other again and rush towards each other and embrace; when I kiss Lisa and press her to my heart— that moment will be the happiest moment of my existence. Lisa is now *free* from all her suffering, her worries and fears; and with her restored hearing, Lisa is able to communicate normally again and enjoy all her favourite music that she was deprived of for the last nine years of her life on Earth.

Lisa was cremated. This was her wish.

May God bless your soul, my dear wife and loyal friend! (*Царство тебе небесное.*)

We are keeping Lisa's ashes at home, so that when I join Lisa, my ashes will be mixed with hers. The beautiful, large Chinese urn was a generous gift from our friend, Tong Wong. Iris and Laura will deposit small amounts of our mixed ashes beneath trees in many of our favourite places and keep the rest at home, which was our most favourite place.

Chapter 35

Ten, Eleven, Twelve—Twenty Months Later

Today is September 6, 2010—ten months since Lisa passed away. I visited the Temple Emanuel synagogue and looked at the plaque that was put up for her in the main hall. When I join Lisa, this plaque will be replaced with a new one, bearing both our names.

I spent about an hour in the synagogue praying. Being Monday, I was the only person there, which was good for me. As I already said in chapter 1, I like praying in Christian churches of any denomination, in Buddhist temples, and in Jewish synagogues, but only on occasions when there are no other people or only very few people present. There is only one God for all of these temples and churches, and it is to Him that my prayers are directed.

I have had no religious upbringing. If all of us would believe in and exercise just one golden rule, "Do unto others as you would have others do unto you," the world would be a much better place—it would be better still if all animals were included in the word *others*. I know that Lisa, Iris, and Laura feel exactly the same way about this. I also know that Laura will bring up her children with that commitment to justice and compassion for all.

Sorry for repeating myself, but this is very important.

Today is the October 6, 2010—eleven months without Lisa at my side. A few days ago, I happened to listen to the reading of Anne Frank's diary on ABC Radio National. This is what this wise-beyond-her-age fourteen-year-old girl said about her widowed grandfather's sadness: she said that for a person in his situation, it is not enough to love and to be loved by other members of his family—he needs to be somebody's one and only.

———————

Next week, it will be twelve months since Lisa passed away. We were informed by the Emanuel Synagogue that Kaddish will be said in remembrance of Lisa during next Friday's service, and that during the Saturday service, on November 6, I will be called up for the reading of two short passages in the Torah. I can read Hebrew and shall do this. The Jewish tradition teaches that through this act, we bring honour to the memory of our loved ones.

———————

Today is the July 6, 2011—twenty months since Lisa and I have been apart—temporarily. When I pray, I ask God to look after Lisa and make sure that she is completely happy, free from all her earthly health burdens, worries, and fears; with restored hearing, able to communicate and to listen to all her favourite Viennese, English, and Hawaiian songs and classical music. I also ask God to allow us to stay together forever after I join Lisa.

On the sixth of every month, we light a candle for Lisa next to the two family photos of the four of us and the lovely photo of Iris and little Laura in Maui, Hawaii. When I sit in front of the candle and these photos, I think of Lisa and look across the lounge room at her empty armchair. When I sit in my study, in front of my computer with the life-size image of Lisa's smiling face on one of the two screens, I often turn my sights towards the door and imagine Lisa entering the room after coming home from her routine household shopping, smiling and saying, "Abale, I'm back. How are you? I'm glad to be home; did you miss me? Can I get you something?" I think to myself, *if only—if only!* I am overcome with feelings of intense longing, combined with deep sadness and loneliness. Thank you, dear God, for the blessing of having such a wife and true friend! I am looking forward to our next happy meeting.

Iris, Laura, and I will always remember, love, and respect Lisa for the precious human being that she was on Earth; her gentle, selfless love for us, her kindness to people and animals, her generosity, and her amazing, selfless courage towards the end of her life.

Laura, please tell your husband/partner about your grandmother, and tell your children about their great-grandmother. Tell them also about me, so that the memory of Lisa and me can live on until, many years from now, we will all be together again.

Until we meet again